MW00628842

Cooking Your Way Across the USA

Poached California Pears — devine!

Printed in the United States of America
by G&R Publishing Co.

Distributed By:

507 Industrial Street
Waverly, IA 50677

ISBN-13: 978-1-56383-337-3
ISBN-10: 1-56383-337-9
Item #7036

Table of Contents

New Harbor, Maine
Lighthouse Lunchbox

Picnic for Four
Spring Crab Dip
Lobster Club with Lemon Mayo
Spinach Salad with Blueberry Dressing
Needhams (Potato Candies)
Whoopie Pies

About Your Destination

New Harbor is a charming fishing village on the Pemaquid Peninsula along the central coast of Maine. Many exciting tours of traditional Maine iconic locations begin here, including the fisherman and artisan island of Monhegan, Pemaquid Point, and Eastern Egg Rock. The area also offers antique shops, farmers markets, a salt pond, and the beautiful coastal waters.

Maine is known for its gorgeous scenery made up of jagged and rocky shores, low rolling mountains and thick lush forestry. The different seasons in Maine are especially marked with wildflowers of spring, the smell of warm salt-air of summer, melting hues of green, yellow and orange leaves of the fall, and brisk skiing in the powdery white snow of winter.

continued

Spring Crab Dip

Makes approximately 3 cups

Ingredients

½ lb. cooked or imitation crabmeat
1 (3 oz.) pkg. cream cheese, softened
½ C. mayonnaise
½ C. sour cream
1½ tsp. lemon juice
Old Bay Seasoning to taste, optional
½ C. chopped green onions
Crackers or raw vegetables to serve

Instructions

Discard any bits of shell or cartilage if
using real crabmeat, or break imitation
crabmeat into smaller pieces; set aside.
In a large bowl, beat together cream
cheese, mayonnaise, sour cream, lemon
juice and if desired, Old Bay Seasoning
until smooth. Stir in green onions and
crabmeat. Chill for 30 minutes before
serving with crackers or raw vegetables.

continued from page 2
Maine is well-known for its
seafood cuisine too – oysters,
crabs and especially clams
and lobsters. Sink your teeth
into some Maine lobster
when you visit coastal
America in New Harbor.

Theme & Setting

Pemaquid Lighthouse rises
above the crash and incredible
rock formations along the
Atlantic Ocean. Featured on
the Maine quarter first released
in 2003, the lighthouse is
one of the most well-known
symbols of Maine today.
The first tower and keeper's
home were built on the
Pemaquid Point in 1827 but
didn't stand for long, as the
builder was suspected to
have used saltwater to mix
the mortar. The second tower
construction, made with no
saltwater, was completed in
1835, and the keeper's house
in 1857. The now-automated
beacon shines 14 miles out to
sea and the keeper's house has
been converted to a museum.

Prepare a Lighthouse
Lunchbox filled with the
culinary delights of Maine.
Then travel to a local pond,
river, lake or ocean shore of
your choosing for a nautical
picnic feast, or bring the
seashore into your home with
shells, clamshell buckets or
nautical colors or emblems.
Serve blueberry wine or
Moxie, the Maine bottled soft
drink that is even celebrated
at the Annual Moxie Festival.

Lobster Club with Lemon Mayo

Makes 4 servings

Ingredients for Lemon Mayo
¾ C. mayonnaise
2 tsp. fresh lemon juice
2 tsp. lemon zest
Pinch of ground black pepper

Ingredients for sandwich
2 C. Maine lobster meat, cooked, thinly sliced*
1 lemon, juiced
Salt and pepper to taste
½ C. minced celery
¼ C. minced green onions
2 T. minced fresh parsley
¾ C. Lemon Mayo, divided
12 slices square sandwich bread, crusts removed, toasted

2 C. baby arugula
2 small tomatoes, thinly sliced
12 slices bacon, cooked
1 ripe avocado, peeled and sliced

Instructions

To make Lemon Mayo: Combine mayonnaise, lemon juice, lemon zest and pepper. Stir until well combined and set aside. **To make lobster spread:** In a large bowl, gently toss lobster meat with lemon juice and salt and pepper to taste. Fold in celery, green onions, parsley and ½ cup Lemon Mayo; set aside. **To build one sandwich:** Spread 1 teaspoon Lemon Mayo on each of 3 slices of toast; place 3 slices of bacon on first slice of toast, followed by tomato slices and arugula leaves; lay second slice of toast on arugula and add avocado slices and ¼ of meat mixture; top the sandwich with final slice of toast, mayo side down. Repeat steps for remaining sandwiches. Secure the layered sandwiches with food picks and cut into 2 triangles to serve.

* See page 6 for instructions on boiling live lobster.

Maine Quick Facts

Date of Statehood:	March 15, 1820
Population:	1,274,923
Capital:	Augusta
State Bird:	Chickadee
State Flower:	White Pine Cone and Tassel
State Nickname:	Pine Tree State

Spinach Salad with Blueberry Dressing

Wild blueberries are one of America's native fruits. Grown on thousands of acres in Maine each year, the state can boast of being the largest producer in the world. Most of Maine's blueberries are frozen or used to make other foods, rather than sold fresh.

Makes 4 servings

Ingredients for dressing

¾ C. fresh or thawed blueberries
¼ C. cider vinegar
1 lemon, juiced
½ tsp. ground mustard
Salt and pepper to taste
¾ C. canola or olive oil

Ingredients for salad

4 C. torn fresh spinach
½ C. fresh or thawed blueberries
½ C. sliced fresh strawberries
⅓ C. thinly sliced red onion
1 T. sunflower seeds
1½ tsp. sesame seeds

Instructions

To make dressing: In a blender, puree berries with vinegar, lemon juice, ground mustard and salt and pepper to taste. Slowly add oil (through the special feed tube or hole in the lid) while blending, until well combined. Refrigerate dressing for 4 to 12 hours before serving. ***To make salad:*** In a large bowl, combine spinach, berries, onion and seeds. Toss with dressing to taste just before serving.

Needhams (Potato Candies)

Thought to have originated in Maine, these candies are now popular throughout New England. Potatoes may seem like an odd ingredient in a candy recipe; however, they are the secret to its sweet success and are part of Maine's agricultural heritage as well.

Makes 24 pieces

Ingredients

¾ C. warm unseasoned mashed potatoes
¼ C. butter, softened
2 lbs. powdered sugar
2 C. sweetened flaked coconut
2 tsp. vanilla extract
½ tsp. salt
12 oz. dark chocolate chips
4 oz. semi-sweet chocolate baking squares

Instructions

In a large mixing bowl, combine mashed potatoes, butter, powdered sugar, coconut, vanilla and salt. Press mixture into a greased 9 x 13˝ pan until firm. Cut into 24 squares. In a microwave or double boiler, melt chocolates. Using a toothpick to hold each candy square, dip squares in chocolate to coat; place on waxed paper to harden. Store in an airtight container.

Whoopie Pies

The whoopie pie is thought by some to have its origin with the Amish of Lancaster County, Pennsylvania, while others argue it was created in Maine. Either way, whoopie pies are a Maine tradition, where they are famously large and more like a cake than a pie or cookie.

<u>Makes 8 servings</u>

Ingredients for cake

2 C. flour
½ C. unsweetened cocoa powder
1¼ tsp. baking soda
1 tsp. salt
½ C. unsalted butter, softened
1 C. brown sugar
1 tsp. vanilla extract

1 egg
1 C. well-shaken buttermilk

Ingredients for filling

½ C. unsalted butter, softened
1¼ C. powdered sugar
2 C. marshmallow crème
1 tsp. vanilla extract

Instructions

Preheat oven to 350°F. **To make cake:** In a large bowl, combine flour, cocoa powder, baking soda and salt; set aside. In a separate large mixing bowl, cream butter and brown sugar for 3 to 5 minutes until pale and fluffy. Add vanilla and egg; beat well. Reduce mixer speed to low and alternately add flour mixture and buttermilk, beating until smooth. Spoon ¼-cup mounds of batter onto well-greased baking sheets with 2″ spacing between mounds. Bake for 11 to 13 minutes until tops are puffed and cakes spring back when touched. Transfer to cooling racks. **To make filling:** Beat butter, powdered sugar, marshmallow crème and vanilla for 3 minutes or until smooth. **To assemble:** When cakes are completely cooled, spoon filling onto flat sides of half the cakes, then top the filling with the remaining cakes, flat side down, to create "sandwich" whoopie pies.

Note: Cakes can be made up to 3 days ahead and stored in an airtight container at room temperature. Filling can be made up to 4 hours ahead and stored at room temperature.

To boil live lobster

Select a stock pot large enough to comfortably hold lobsters; do not crowd them. Fill empty pot with water, allowing 3 quarts for each 1½ to 2 pounds of lobster. Add ¼ cup sea salt for each gallon of water used. Bring water to a rolling boil, then add live lobsters one at a time and start timing immediately; do not cover pot. Cook for approximately 1 minute per 2 ounces of lobster weight. For example, if lobsters weigh 1 pound each, boil for 8 minutes; or if lobsters weigh 2 pounds each, boil pot of lobsters for 16 minutes. Stir halfway through cooking. Remove lobsters from water and allow to stand for 5 minutes before serving.

Food for Thought

- Maine seafood has attained an almost a cult-like status, as the deep, cold waters seem to be the best for quality and freshness. Maine takes great pride in its ocean and farm-raised seafood offerings of lobster, clams, oysters, mussels, bay scallops and more.

- Lobster and clam bakes take place on the shores of Maine, where driftwood fires are stoked in fire pits built on the sand with cinder blocks. Fresh lobsters and clams are boiled on site in washtubs lined with seaweed and enjoyed in the earthy presence of nature and friends.

- Other important commodities harvested in Maine include poultry, eggs, potatoes, blueberries, apples, maple syrup, and beef and dairy products.

While in the Area

- Dig clams in the prime clam digging grounds of the Maine coastline. You just need to pick up a clamming license for the day and ask for directions. Then head out during low tide, walk around and look for holes in the mud. Be sure to wear some gloves and dig enough for dinner.

- Search for magical sea glass in the sands of Maine's shorelines. The treasures are actually broken pieces of bottles and jars that have been sanded to a fine frosty finish by the abrasion of rocks, sand and water. Many different colors are produced by the ocean tides and are crafted into unique pieces of jewelry by Maine artisans.

- Learn a lesson of love from some true "love birds," the Atlantic Puffins. Remarkable loyalty and life-long mating are the way of life for these orange-beaked, black and white seabirds. Heavily hunted along the Maine coast in the 19th century, it is believed that by 1901, only one pair remained. Efforts have been made toward repopulation of the birds in New England, and today, pairs of puffins can be seen from boats as they travel along the rocky shores of Eastern Egg Island.

Nantucket, Massachusetts
Dinner at the Summer Beach House

Dinner for Six to Eight
Pan-Fried Scallops
Crab Melt Bites
Nantucket Baked Cod
Lemon Roasted Baby Carrots & Potatoes
Fluffy Cranberry Mousse
Fizzy Cranberry Lemonade

About your Destination

Off the coast of Massachusetts, the charming Nantucket Island is a popular vacation spot that offers an unforgettable, quiet and casual escape from daily life on the mainland. Nantucket is the name of the sound, the island, the county and the main village on the Island. Guests arrive by ferry or by plane, to be greeted by their hosts, as well as handfuls of artists and writers who call the Island home. The rich history of the Island, once the whaling capital of the world, comes alive as visitors walk the cobblestone streets and enter the historic structures; some date as far back as the late 1600s.

Americana beach and maritime charm work their way into the hearts of visitors as they shop in the fishing village, take a ride out to sea, or bike to a beach. With miles of sand and dunes,

continued

Pan-Fried Scallops

Makes 8 appetizer servings

Ingredients

⅓ C. flour
1 tsp. salt
½ tsp. dried oregano
2 T. lemon pepper
1 lb. cleaned sea scallops
4 T. olive oil, divided
4 T. chopped fresh parsley, divided
1 lemon, cut in wedges

Instructions

Combine flour, salt, oregano and lemon pepper in a large sealable plastic bag. Add scallops, seal the bag and gently toss ingredients until scallops are evenly coated. Empty scallops onto a platter; discard plastic bag and flour. Preheat medium skillet over medium-high heat for 1 minute. Add 2 tablespoons oil and heat for 1 additional minute. Working in two batches, use tongs to gently shake excess flour from scallops and place them in the skillet. Brown scallops on each side for 2 minutes until a golden brown crust has formed on the outside and flesh is warmed through. Remove and place scallops onto a clean serving platter that has been evenly sprinkled with 2 tablespoons of parsley. Carefully wipe out the inside of the skillet and heat remaining 2 tablespoons oil for 1 minute. Complete the cooking process for remaining scallops. Plate the second batch of scallops with the first. Sprinkle remaining 2 tablespoons parsley over the scallops and garnish with lemon wedges to serve.

continued from page 8
and numerous beaches labeled with names such as Jetties, Cisco and Great Point, there is sure to be a special spot to dub as your "favorite."

Theme & Setting

Make your way up from the beach to dry off with a towel and warm up to a home-cooked dinner. The menu creates a palate of summer tastes as you decorate with a palate of inviting ocean colors. Coordinated crisp whites and cool blues will set off the dining table. Place votive candles throughout the room for a warm glow as the sun begins to fade. A casual centerpiece of small pails and shells or smooth stones will make it seem like the kids were just out combing the beach for treasures; or try a tall skinny vase of wispy grasses that will make you feel like they were just plucked from the sand dunes of Nantucket Island. Invite friends to have dinner in your "Summer Beach House" for a memorable evening along the shores of Nantucket Island.

Crab Melt Bites

Makes 24 appetizers

Ingredients

½ C. sharp Cheddar cheese spread
¼ C. butter, softened
1 T. mayonnaise
⅛ tsp. garlic powder
¼ tsp. seasoned salt
1 C. cooked or imitation crabmeat
3 regular-size English muffins, split
Paprika

Instructions

In a medium bowl, combine cheese spread, butter, mayonnaise, garlic powder and seasoned salt; mix until smooth. Discard any bits of shell or cartilage if using real crabmeat, or break imitation crabmeat into smaller pieces. Gently fold crabmeat into cheese mixture. Spread crabmeat mixture on muffin halves and sprinkle with paprika. Cut each half into quarters. Place quarters onto a baking sheet with crabmeat mixture face-up. Cover with plastic wrap and place in freezer for 20 minutes. Preheat oven to 350°F. Remove plastic wrap and bake for 20 minutes until browned and bubbly. Serve hot.

Nantucket Baked Cod

Makes 6 servings

Ingredients

3 lbs. fresh or frozen, thawed cod fish fillets
2 T. butter, melted
1 lemon, halved for juicing
½ tsp. salt
½ tsp. paprika
⅛ tsp. ground black pepper
⅛ tsp. cayenne pepper
3 small tomatoes, thinly sliced
¼ C. grated Parmesan cheese
8 lemon wedges, optional

Instructions

Preheat oven to 425°F. Cut cod into 8-ounce serving size portions; overlap two smaller pieces to form a full portion if necessary. Arrange six servings of cod in a 9 x 13″ baking dish. Brush top of each serving with butter and then squeeze lemon juice on top. In a small bowl, combine salt, paprika, black pepper and cayenne pepper. Sprinkle spice mixture evenly over the fish. Arrange 2 to 3 tomato slices on top of each serving; sprinkle with Parmesan. Bake fish, uncovered, for 10 minutes; turn oven to broil and continue to cook for 6 to 8 minutes or until cheese and tomato begin to brown and fish is cooked through. If desired, serve with lemon wedges.

Lemon Roasted Baby Carrots & Potatoes

The near absence of clay in the soil of Nantucket allows for the formation of excellent root vegetables such as straight carrots and almost perfect radishes and potatoes.

Makes 8 servings

Ingredients

2 lbs. white boiling potatoes, peeled and cut into ¾˝ cubes, or small red potatoes, halved or quartered if large

2 lbs. baby carrots*

½ C. fresh lemon juice

2 T. chopped fresh oregano

½ C. chopped fresh parsley

½ C. olive oil

Salt and pepper to taste

Paprika, optional

Instructions

Place potatoes and carrots in a large stock pot and cover with salted water. Bring to a boil over high heat and continue to boil for 5 minutes or until slightly softened. Drain and transfer vegetables to a large bowl. Toss with lemon juice and let stand for 15 minutes. Preheat oven 450°F. Sprinkle vegetables with oregano, parsley, oil and salt and pepper to taste. Transfer to a shallow baking dish and roast, stirring occasionally, for 35 minutes or until tender and potatoes are golden. If desired, sprinkle with paprika before serving hot.

*Thick baby carrots can be sliced lengthwise to cook more quickly and evenly.

Massachusetts Quick Facts

Date of Statehood:	February 6, 1788
Population:	6,349,097
Capital:	Boston
State Bird:	Chickadee
State Flower:	Mayflower
State Nickname:	Bay State

Fluffy Cranberry Mousse

Cranberries, grown on Nantucket since the mid 1800s, were an important part of Nantucket's economy until just before WWII. Two commercial bogs remain on the island where cranberries are a traditional favorite.

Makes 8 servings

Ingredients

1 C. fresh cranberries

⅓ C. plus 2 T. sugar, divided

2 T. water

½ (8 oz.) pkg. cream cheese, softened

½ tsp. vanilla extract

½ C. frozen cranberry juice concentrate, thawed

1 (16 oz.) can whole cranberry sauce

1½ C. heavy whipping cream

Instructions

To make sweetened cranberries: In a medium skillet, combine cranberries, ⅓ cup sugar and water. Over medium heat, cook until sugar is dissolved and cranberries just begin to pop. Remove from heat, cover and chill until cold, for serving. **To make mousse:** In a large mixing bowl, beat cream cheese on medium speed for 30 seconds. Add remaining 2 tablespoons sugar and vanilla; beat until smooth. Slowly add cranberry concentrate and continue to beat until smooth. Set cream cheese mixture aside. In a small bowl, stir whole cranberry sauce to remove any large lumps. In a separate chilled medium mixing bowl, beat whipping cream on medium speed until soft peaks form. Gently fold half of the whipped cream and half of the cranberry sauce into the cream cheese mixture until just combined; repeat with remaining whipped cream and cranberry sauce. Serve immediately or cover and store in the refrigerator for up to 24 hours. Stir well before serving if chilled. **To serve:** Spoon cranberry mousse into dessert dishes and top with sweetened cranberries.

Fizzy Cranberry Lemonade

Makes 8 servings

Ingredients

4 C. cranberry juice cocktail

1 (6 oz.) can frozen lemonade concentrate, thawed

4 C. club soda or ginger ale

1 small orange

Ice cubes

Instructions

In a large pitcher, stir together cranberry juice cocktail and undiluted lemonade concentrate until well blended. Stir in club soda or ginger ale. Wash and slice orange into 8 wedges; place 1 wedge in each serving glass with ice. Pour lemonade over ice and oranges to serve.

Food for Thought

- Although only a handful of Nantucket fishers earn a living by commercial fishing, the waters are rich with sea bass, tuna, bluefish and more. Nantucket Bay Scallops are famous and considered by many gourmets to be the finest of the five eastern species, juicier and sweeter than the others.

- Nantucket is home to several small wineries and host to the annual Nantucket Wine Festival which invites more than 100 of the world's great wineries to pour at the Grand Tasting. The festival also features food and wine seminars, a symposium, a luncheon and a gala.

- Family-owned farms dot the land, making fresh fruits and vegetables available to Nantucket residents and visitors. Farmers and artisans markets display the wide variety of corn, tomatoes, radishes, berries and other organic produce. Herbs, plants and cut flowers, as well as hand-crafted pottery, jewelry, crafts and more are also available.

While in the Area

- Pedal your bike leisurely over the island as you enjoy ocean views alongside the beaches, lighthouses, grassy dunes and cranberry bogs. Nantucket's small size and flat terrain make it ideal for relaxed rides in natural beauty.

- Become an owner of a piece of unique artwork when you attend one of the numerous events held in conjunction with the annual Fall Arts Festival held in Nantucket. The festival features shows and entertainment, art gallery showcases and even a parade.

- Learn of maritime life with visits to the Nantucket Aquarium and the Nantucket Whaling Museum. The aquarium offers an abundance of information on the aquatic life found in the Nantucket saltwater marshes. The museum features a restored candle factory, lighthouse artifacts, a rooftop observation deck overlooking the harbor, and even a 46-foot skeleton of a whale.

Lancaster, Pennsylvania
Simply Amish

Dinner for Six to Eight
Best Broccoli Salad
No-Knead Overnight Dinner Rolls
Farmer's Meatloaf
Escalloped Potatoes
Jonathan Apple Pie

Another Taste of Pennsylvania
Amish Caramel Corn

About your Destination

Lancaster is just one of a number of historic villages tucked away like treasure in Lancaster County, Pennsylvania. With many towns dating back to the early 1700s, the county is most well-known for being situated in the heart of Pennsylvania Dutch country, where more than 25 different Amish, Mennonite and Brethren Churches make their home. A trip down dusty roads and over covered bridges reveals horses working croplands, farmsteads with plain white houses, clotheslines of breeze-dried laundry and enormous barns raised by the hands of neighbors and friends. Further down the road is a one-room schoolhouse where children play simple games during recess. Electrical poles and lines are absent, as the Amish choose to live without electricity, cars and other things

continued

14

Best Broccoli Salad

Makes 8 to 10 servings

Ingredients

1 large bunch broccoli,
    cut into bite-sized florets
1 C. chopped celery
⅔ C. toasted slivered almonds*
1 C. red grapes, halved
1 C. green grapes, halved
8 slices bacon, cooked and
    crumbled
½ C. chopped green onions
1 C. Miracle Whip salad dressing
1 T. vinegar
½ C. brown sugar

Instructions

In a large bowl, combine broccoli, celery, almonds, grapes, bacon and green onions. In a medium bowl, whisk salad dressing, vinegar and brown sugar until smooth. Fold dressing into broccoli mixture and stir until evenly coated. Serve immediately.

Note: Ingredients and dressing can be prepared in advance, chilled and then combined just before serving.

*To toast, place almonds in a single layer on a baking sheet. Bake at 350°F for approximately 5 to 10 minutes or until almonds are golden brown.

continued from page 14
considered necessary by outsiders. The Amish are very devout in their faith, which serves as a guide for their simple and separate lifestyle.

Amish humility is displayed in the appearance and style of self and home. Solid-colored fabrics are sewn into long-sleeved dresses with full skirts, simple suits and shirts. Most often, women wear their uncut hair in buns with a head covering and men wear suspenders and broad-brimmed black or straw hats. Homes are plain too, with wood furnishings and floors, cook stoves and generous dining tables to seat the members of their large families. A good-sized open living room can accommodate church services. Amish simplicity goes hand in hand with their strong sense of community, family and faith.

Theme & Setting

Let the image of a simple Amish dinner table guide you as you prepare a "Simply Amish" meal tonight. Select fresh ingredients from your local grocer, farmers market or garden. A sunny red potted geranium makes an excellent country centerpiece and plates piled high with home-cookin' complete the setting. Although there are occasional quilting bees, formal gatherings, or trips to farm shows, the most popular leisure activity for the Amish seems to be visiting. Sit back and enjoy a simple meal and simple times while you visit with friends and family.

No-Knead Overnight Dinner Rolls

Makes 2½ dozen

Ingredients

2 (.75 oz.) pkgs. active dry yeast
1¼ C. very warm water, divided
3 large eggs
5 C. unbleached flour, divided
½ C. sugar
¾ C. butter, melted, divided
2 tsp. salt
¼ C. softened butter

Instructions

Sprinkle both packages of yeast into ¼ cup of very warm water and stir with a fork; set aside for 10 minutes. In a large mixing bowl, beat eggs and blend in dissolved yeast. Add 2½ cups flour, alternating with remaining 1 cup very warm water. Add sugar, ½ cup melted butter and salt and mix until smooth. Beat in remaining flour to make a soft dough, cover with a tea towel and place in a warm and draft-free place; let rise for 1 to 2 hours until doubled in size. Punch dough down, cover with plastic wrap and refrigerate overnight. Grease muffin tins.

Punch dough down again and divide in half. On a lightly floured surface, roll out each half into an 8 x 15˝ rectangle. Spread with ¼ cup softened butter. Starting with the long edge, roll up dough jelly-roll fashion. With a sharp knife, cut into 1˝ slices. Lay one slice, flat, in each cup of the muffin tins. Let rise for 40 to 60 minutes until doubled in size. Preheat oven to 400°F. Bake for 8 to 10 minutes or until golden brown. Immediately brush with remaining ¼ cup melted butter and place on a rack to cool. Serve with butter and/or strawberry jam.

Farmer's Meatloaf

Makes 6 to 8 servings

Ingredients

1½ lbs. ground beef
½ tsp. onion salt
1⅓ C. cracker crumbs
1 C. milk
1 large egg, lightly beaten
1 C. ketchup
⅓ C. brown sugar
1½ tsp. vinegar
3 T. Worcestershire sauce

Pennsylvania Quick Facts

Date of Statehood:	December 12, 1787
Population:	12,281,054
Capital:	Harrisburg
State Bird:	Ruffed Grouse
State Flower:	Mountain Laurel
State Nickname:	Keystone State

Instructions

In a large bowl, combine ground beef, onion salt, cracker crumbs, milk and egg; stir until well blended. Pat mixture into a 5 x 9 x 3″ loaf pan. Preheat oven to 350°F. In a saucepan, combine ketchup, brown sugar, vinegar and Worcestershire sauce. Cook and stir over medium heat for 5 to 10 minutes or until bubbly. Pour sauce over meat. Bake for 1 hour and 15 minutes. Let rest for 5 to 10 minutes and slice to serve.

Escalloped Potatoes

Makes 8 large servings

Ingredients

8 large potatoes, peeled and sliced (about 8 C.)
¼ C. flour
¼ C. finely minced fresh parsley
Salt and pepper to taste
Ground nutmeg, optional
½ C. butter
2½ C. milk
¼ tsp. paprika

Instructions

Preheat oven to 325°F. Grease a 9 x 13″ (or similar size) baking dish. Create three layers of potatoes and seasoning; start with a layer of potatoes, sprinkle lightly with a portion of flour, a portion of parsley, salt, pepper and if desired, nutmeg to taste. Repeat with remaining potatoes, flour and seasonings to taste. In a small saucepan, heat butter and milk together over low heat until just warm, not boiling. Pour warm milk mixture over potatoes. Sprinkle with paprika. Bake for 1½ hours or until top is golden brown and potatoes are tender.

Jonathan Apple Pie

The Amish are justifiably famous for their pies, including some with very unique names or flavors such as Bob Andy Pie, Cottage Cheese Pie, Brown Sugar Pie and Lemon Sponge Pie. Apple desserts are a favorite, so this pie featuring homegrown Jonathans is perfect for a Simply Amish meal.

Makes 8 pieces

Ingredients

1½ C. plus 3 T. flour, divided
½ tsp. salt
½ C. plus 2 T. vegetable shortening
¼ C. cold water
6 to 7 C. peeled and sliced Jonathan apples
½ tsp. ground cinnamon
¾ C. sugar
2 T. butter, cut into small chunks
Sugar and ground cinnamon to taste
Vanilla ice cream, optional

Instructions

In a medium bowl, combine 1½ cups flour with salt; cut in shortening with a fork or pastry blender until well combined and crumbly. Blend in water with a fork to form dough. Divide dough in half. On a lightly floured work surface, roll half of dough to form a bottom crust large enough to cover the bottom of a 9″ pie plate. To move dough to pie plate, gently

continued

continued from page 17

fold it in half to handle; lay it over the pie plate, unfolding and letting extra dough fall over the edge. Add apples to pie plate. Sprinkle with remaining 3 tablespoons flour, cinnamon and sugar. Dot with chunks of butter. Preheat oven to 400°F. Repeat rolling process for top crust; place it gently over the apples. Pinch outside crusts of pie together, removing any excess dough from the outer edge. Sprinkle top crust with cinnamon and sugar to taste. With a sharp knife, cut 8 to 10 slits in the top crust. Bake for 20 minutes, then reduce temperature to 350°F and bake for 40 additional minutes or until crust is golden and apples are soft. Lay narrow strips of foil over outside edges of crust during the last 15 minutes of baking to protect it from over-browning. Cut into wedges and if desired, serve with vanilla ice cream.

*Jonathan apples are best, but if unavailable, substitute Granny Smith or another sweet-tart baking apple.

Amish Caramel Corn

Makes 6 quarts

Ingredients

6 qts. popped corn, lightly salted
1 C. butter
2 C. brown sugar
½ C. light corn syrup
1 tsp. baking soda

Instructions

Preheat oven to 200°F. Select a roasting pan large enough to allow room for thorough stirring while baking; place popped corn in the pan. In a large saucepan, melt butter over medium-high heat. Add brown sugar and corn syrup; bring to a boil, stirring constantly. Boil for 5 minutes, stirring constantly. Remove from heat and immediately stir in baking soda; the mixture will foam up and almost double in size. Pour hot mixture over popped corn and mix well. Bake for 1 hour, stirring well every 15 minutes during baking. Remove from oven to cool, stirring occasionally, until completely cool. Store in an airtight container.

Food for Thought

- Gardens and orchards feature a magnificent assortment of fruits and vegetables from spring through fall. Seeking variety, Amish families not only plant familiar tomatoes, green beans and cabbages, but also red Swiss chard, tiny beets, eggplants, sugar snap peas and much more.

- Because the Amish have chosen to remain separate from the rest of society, much of their cuisine remains unchanged over the years. Many cooks continue to prepare dishes as their European ancestors did.

- Canning is an essential skill and activity of the Amish women. In each home, hundreds of jars of preserved fruits, vegetables and meats will be stored up for the long winter. With heavy German influence, kraut-making is a big fall tradition.

- The Amish are noted for their baking skills. Young girls learn how to make a pie crust from their mothers. There is no recipe... they are so familiar with the process, they just mix lard and flour and add a little water.

While in the Area

- Hire a horse and buggy to take you for a ride. Many Amish-themed attractions are available, like rides in the traditional horse-drawn black buggies, or tours of the Amish Farm and House, a working farm complete with farm animals.

- Bite into a piece of chocolate when you travel nine miles outside the county to nearby Hershey, Pennsylvania. Milton Hershey built his chocolate empire here, where kiss-shaped streetlights line the streets and the never-ending smell of chocolate fills the air. Visit the Hershey factory or the amusement park for extra sweet times.

- Purchase a piece of American artwork, an Amish quilt. While clothing is plain, the quilts are often bright colors set against a pattern of contrasting black fabric. Traditionally, Amish women enjoy gathering at a quilting bee to quilt as a group. After piecing a quilt, a hostess invites friends and neighbors to gather around the quilt frame to stitch as they share news and stories. Quilting has become a cottage industry for some. Quilt-making, as well as other artisian trades such as furniture making, not only provide an additional income source for the Amish, but a way for outsiders to enjoy their fine handiwork.

- Visit Bird-in-Hand, Manheim, Columbia, Lititz or one of the other small towns of Lancaster County to see early American log cabins, Victorian homes and Art Deco architecture, as well as unique pieces of American history, like America's first pretzel factory.

Traverse City, Michigan
Gone Fishin' - Friday Night Fish Fry

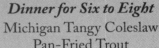

Dinner for Six to Eight
Michigan Tangy Coleslaw
Pan-Fried Trout
Easiest Hot Applesauce
Creamy Baked Macaroni & Cheese
All-American Cherry Pie

Another Taste of Michigan
Mackinac Island Famous Fudge

About your Destination

The state of Michigan has been blessed with the riches of unspoiled nature. The world's longest freshwater coastline is claimed by Michigan, with exposure to four of the five Great Lakes which feel more like ocean than pond. Travel through miles of cherry orchards, witness amazing sunrises and sunsets and take in other natural wonders that will make you feel like you entered a paradise. The Upper Peninsula, thick with forest, sees more than 300 inches of snow annually, making it a white wonderland for winter sports enthusiasts. But Michigan is not just for winter sports; other seasons offer pastimes such as camping, golfing, boating and watching the turning colors of fall foliage.

continued

Michigan Tangy Coleslaw

This recipe takes advantage of Michigan apples and cherries, combined in a famous fried-fish accompaniment, coleslaw.

Makes 8 servings

Ingredients

½ C. mayonnaise

¼ C. lemon juice

2 T. sugar

Salt to taste

¼ C. water

2 (10 oz.) pkgs. shredded cabbage coleslaw mix

2 large carrots, peeled and grated

4 green onions, thinly sliced

½ C. dried cherries, coarsely chopped

½ C. chopped tart apples

½ C. chopped walnuts, optional

Instructions

In a small bowl, whisk together mayonnaise, lemon juice, sugar, salt and water. In a large bowl, combine cabbage mix, carrots, green onions, cherries, apples and, if desired, walnuts. Add dressing and toss well to coat. Refrigerate for 2 hours before serving.

continued from page 20

Traverse City, which rests along Michigan's northern coast, has been described as a four-season playground for anyone who loves the great outdoors. From here you can hike a lonely sand beach or quiet wooded trail, climb a windswept dune to peer over the endless blue of Lake Michigan, or try your hand at fishing. Traverse City has a beautiful marina, quaint shops and excellent golf courses as well.

Theme & Setting

"Gone Fishin": two little words that speak volumes about the passion for spending time in fresh air and on the water in the effort to "land the big one." Besides the Great Lakes, the miles of rivers and abundant small lakes make fishing a popular past-time. Trout and salmon fly-fishing are popular in Michigan, where the Brook Trout is a state symbol. Even if you don't catch one yourself, gather with friends to enjoy a feast of fish, and savor the fact that someone else has gone fishin'.

In Northern Michigan, nothing says Friday like a fish fry. Hungry people line up outside town halls and local taverns like clockwork during Lenten season. Keep it casual as you decorate for your Fish Fry, with red checkered or cherry print tablecloths. Have frosty mugs of root beer and plenty of paper napkins. Make fish-shaped placemats out of cardstock or butcher paper and provide crayons for guests to doodle while they wait for the "catch of the day."

Pan-Fried Trout

Deep-fried cod or perch are often served for a large-group fish fry, but this pan-fried recipe works well for enjoying the local trout of Michigan.
Makes 8 servings

Ingredients

1 C. flour or cornmeal
4 tsp. dried parsley flakes
2 tsp. dried minced onions
2 tsp. garlic powder
2 tsp. dried basil
1 tsp. salt
½ tsp. dried lemon peel
½ tsp. ground black pepper
Pinch of cayenne pepper
4 (9 oz.) trout, cleaned and filleted
2 T. cooking oil
Lemon wedges, optional

Instructions

In a large sealable plastic bag, combine first 9 ingredients; seal and shake to blend. Add pieces of fish to the bag, several at a time, and gently shake to coat. In a large heavy skillet, heat oil over medium heat. Cook coated fish for 6 minutes per side, or until flaky and cooked through. If desired, garnish with lemon wedges before serving.

Easiest Hot Applesauce

Makes 6 servings

Ingredients

6 medium-sized sweet apples*, peeled, cored and quartered
1 C. unfiltered apple juice
2 T. butter
3 T. honey
½ tsp. ground cinnamon
2 T. cognac or brandy, optional
Brown sugar, optional

Instructions

In a microwave-safe container with a lid, combine apples, juice, butter, honey, cinnamon and, if desired, cognac or brandy. Cover the container loosely, to allow some steam to escape. Microwave on high for 10 minutes, stirring occasionally. With a hand blender or potato masher, blend apple mixture to desired consistency. If desired, sprinkle lightly with brown sugar. Serve immediately or refrigerate for later use.

*A combination of Golden Delicious, Fuji or Gala apples works nicely.

Michigan Quick Facts

Date of Statehood:	January 26, 1837
Population:	9,938,444
Capital:	Lansing
State Bird:	Robin
State Flower:	Apple Blossom
State Nickname:	Wolverine State/Great Lakes State

Creamy Baked Macaroni & Cheese

Makes 6 servings

Ingredients

2 C. uncooked elbow macaroni
¼ C. butter or margarine, melted
¼ C. flour
½ tsp. salt
¼ tsp. ground black pepper
¼ tsp. ground mustard
¼ tsp. Worcestershire sauce
2 C. milk
2 C. shredded sharp Cheddar
cheese

Instructions

Preheat oven to 350°F. Cook macaroni according to package directions; rinse, drain and set aside. In a large saucepan over medium-low heat, melt butter. Stir in flour, salt, pepper, mustard and Worcestershire sauce. Cook while stirring, until smooth and bubbly. Stir in milk and heat to boiling; continue to stir and boil for 1 minute. Add cheese and stir until melted; remove from heat. Combine macaroni with the cheese mixture and pour into a 2-quart baking dish. Bake uncovered for 20 to 25 minutes or until bubbly.

All-American Cherry Pie

Makes 8 pieces

Ingredients

4 C. tart cherries, pitted
1½ tsp. lemon juice
1⅓ C. sugar
2 T. tapioca
2 T. cornstarch
Pastry for double-crust 9″ pie
2 T. butter, cut into small chunks
Milk for basting
Sugar for sprinkling
Special equipment – lattice crust
cutter, optional

Instructions

In a large bowl, combine cherries, lemon juice, sugar, tapioca and cornstarch; stir until well mixed. Lay bottom crust in a 9″ pie plate and spoon cherry mixture on top. Dot with chunks of butter. Preheat oven to 400°F. Using a knife or if desired, a lattice crust cutter, cut top crust and place it over cherry mixture in a lattice pattern. Lightly brush crust with milk and sprinkle lightly with sugar. Bake for 15 minutes, then reduce heat to 350°F and bake for 35 to 40 additional minutes. Lay narrow strips of foil over outside edges of crust during the last 15 minutes of baking to protect it from over-browning. Cut into wedges to serve.

Mackinac Island Famous Fudge

Mackinac Island lies just to the east of the enormous Mackinac Bridge, the third largest suspension bridge in the world. It reaches almost five miles to connect the Lower and Upper Peninsulas of Michigan. An Americana icon, Mackinac Island is home to quaint bed and breakfasts, horse-drawn carriages and bicycles (no cars are allowed on the Island), the famous Grand Hotel, and a variety of shops. Fudge, made by the candy makers of Mackinac, makes the sweetest Michigan souvenir. Although you can only get authentic Mackinac Island fudge by visiting the island, this recipe will give you a taste of the treasure in store.

Makes approximately 3 pounds

Ingredients

3 C. sugar

¾ C. margarine

1 (5 oz.) can evaporated milk

1 (12 oz.) pkg. semi-sweet chocolate chips

1 (7 oz.) jar marshmallow crème

1 C. chopped nuts

1 tsp. vanilla extract

Special equipment – candy thermometer

Instructions

Line a 9″ x 13″ baking dish with foil, extending the foil over the edges of the pan. Butter the foil; set pan aside. In a heavy 2- to 3-quart saucepan, combine sugar, margarine and milk. Bring to a full rolling boil, stirring constantly. Continue boiling for 5 minutes over medium heat or until candy thermometer reaches 234°F, stirring constantly to prevent scorching. Remove from heat and stir in chocolate pieces until melted. Add marshmallow crème, nuts and vanilla; beat until well blended. Spread in prepared dish. Cool at room temperature. When firm, lift foil from pan and cut into squares to serve.

Food for Thought

- Since Michigan is home to dozens of ethnic groups with no clear "cuisine" of its own, Michigan's food is described by "foodway," or local and regional specialty groupings. The important thing to note about Michigan cuisine is that it is down-to-earth and features locally harvested or hunted ingredients.

- A variety of Michigan foods are celebrated with festivals throughout the year. From the Walleye Festival to the Maple Syrup Festival, from the National Asparagus Festival to a number of Strawberry Festivals, and from the Bologna Festival to the Pickle Festival, there is always an abundance of reasons to gather in the name of food.

- One regional specialty is the "pasty" of the Upper Peninsula. Basically, individual pies are filled with meats and vegetables and cooked together, similar to turnovers or pot-pies, but without the pot.

- Traverse City is home to wineries which are quickly becoming nationally and internationally known. Rieslings, Chardonnays, fruit wines and Pinot Noirs are bottled in Michigan.

While in the Area

- Descend from the top of the dunes at Sleeping Bear Dunes National Lakeshore to the waters of Lake Michigan. The hike is almost unbelievably steep and best traversed by those feeling youthful or especially energetic. From the top of the dunes, the view is magnificent as you look westward over the deep blue waters of Lake Michigan.

- Spit a pit after biting into the ripe summer cherries of Northern Michigan. The cherry industry in Michigan dates back to the 1800s and now provides more than two-thirds of the tart cherries grown in the United States. The tart cherries are mainly grown for pies, preserves, jellies, juice and dried fruits, rather than for fresh eating.

- View some of the best show jumping in the nation, as competitors take part in the Horse Shows by the Bay Equestrian Festival held at Flintfields Horse Park in Traverse City.

Pulaski, Wisconsin
Oom Pah Pah Polka Party

Casual Dinner or Lunch for Eight
Creamy Brick Spread
Wisconsin Beer Cheese Soup
Wisconsin Beer Brats
German Potato Salad
Fresh Orchard Apple Crisp
Spiced Apple Cider

About your Destination

The colors of Wisconsin are stunning. Crisp white snow blankets (and sometimes buries) the wide winter landscape. The bright green of the first spring growth turns to deep rich green lasting throughout the summer. And finally, a canopy of leaves turns gold, red, orange, rust, brown and every shade in between, as the seasons come full circle again. The colorful imagery of Wisconsin's scenery is just one piece of the picture; Wisconsin is represented by many interesting and unique symbols. Rural symbols include dairy cows, cheese, cranberries and snowmobiling, while Wisconsin's urban symbols include major breweries, Harley Davidson and the Green Bay Packers.

Drive a few miles outside of Green Bay and you will arrive in the small "Polish" town of Pulaski, home to one of the largest polka festivals in the

continued

Creamy Brick Spread

Brick cheese, a Wisconsin original, is named not only for its brick-like shape, but also for the fact that bricks were used by the original cheesemakers to press moisture from the cheese. Young brick cheese is mild and creamy, while well-aged cheese is dense and pungent.

<u>Makes 1½ cups</u>

Ingredients

8 oz. Wisconsin brick cheese, shredded

1 (8 oz.) pkg. cream cheese

1 T. chopped fresh chives

2 T. minced fresh onion

½ tsp. hot pepper sauce

Pumpernickel, rye or wheat breads, crisps or crackers

Instructions

In a large mixing bowl, blend brick cheese, cream cheese, chives, onion and hot pepper sauce until smooth. Serve with bread or crackers.

continued from page 26

U.S. Numerous polka bands in this small town have some locals boasting that it is home to more bands per capita than even Nashville. Polka is big in Wisconsin – so big that it has been named the official dance of the state and you can hear the lively music played on local radio stations.

Theme & Setting

Polka rose out of rural Europe during the 1840s. The Bohemian dance is thought to have been started by a peasant girl who invented the steps one day for her own amusement. Soon it was introduced in Prague, Paris and elsewhere in Europe, and as immigrants made their way to U.S. soil, they brought the polka with them, where it has become a piece of American history and culture. Very popular with the Polish, the polka was also a favorite of Czech and German immigrants. Classic polka seems to never go out of style while newer polkas develop, such as the Texas polka and punk polka.

Hosting an "Oom Pah Pah" Polka Party is a fantastic way to feature the foods that make up Wisconsin cuisine. Listen to polka music as you eat, and after dinner, spend time learning or teaching the polka. Be sure to include familiar favorites such as the Chicken Dance and the Beer Barrel Polka. Party favors of European-styled hats and pretty aprons with floral stitching can double as "costumes" for your guests. Décor suggestions, with a Polish, German or Czechoslovakian twist, include potted flowers in window boxes or little figurine knick-knacks. Fill beer steins with fresh cut flowers, or make centerpieces out of cutting boards topped with cheese and crackers, grapes, sausage, apples and a small dish of Creamy Brick Spread. Tuck pieces of polka sheet music under or around the board.

Wisconsin Beer Cheese Soup

Numerous microbreweries, as well as the major producers, contribute to making Wisconsin the "Beer Capital of the United States." Many different dishes are prepared using beer, but Wisconsin Beer Cheese Soup has to be one of the best-known Wisconsin culinary creations.

<u>*Makes 8 servings*</u>

Ingredients

¼ C. butter
⅓ C. chopped green onions
¼ C. finely chopped carrot
¼ C. finely chopped cabbage
¼ C. flour
2½ C. chicken broth
½ C. beer*
1 T. Dijon mustard
2 C. half & half
2 C. shredded aged Wisconsin Cheddar cheese

Instructions

In a large heavy pan over medium-high heat, melt butter. Add onions, carrots and cabbage; sauté while stirring until vegetables are translucent. Stir in flour and cook for 1 minute, stirring constantly.

Add broth, beer and mustard; continue to stir until mixture reaches a boil. Reduce heat to low, cover and simmer for 30 minutes. In a small saucepan or microwave, heat half & half until almost boiling. Add hot half & half and cheese to soup mixture; stir over low heat until cheese is melted and soup is heated through.

*Additional half & half or chicken broth can be substituted for beer.

Wisconsin Beer Brats

<u>*Makes 10 servings*</u>

Ingredients

10 fresh bratwurst
6 bottles or cans of beer, divided
2 large onions, chopped, divided
10 crusty hoagie rolls or brat buns
Assorted condiments: dill pickle spears, warmed sauerkraut, ketchup, brown mustard, chopped onions

Instructions

If cooking with charcoal, prepare grill. Meanwhile, place the brats in a large pot and add half the beer, half the onions and just enough water to cover brats.

Wisconsin Quick Facts

Date of Statehood:	May 29, 1848
Population:	5,363,675
Capital:	Madison
State Bird:	Robin
State Flower:	Wood Violet
State Nickname:	Badger State

WISCONSIN

1848

Over high heat, bring mixture to a boil; reduce heat and continue to simmer for 20 minutes. Meanwhile, preheat gas grill, and combine remaining beer and onions in an oven- or grill-safe container to use as a holding liquid for grilled brats; set aside. Drain brats and discard boiling mixture. Grill brats, turning often, until nicely browned and cooked through. (The bratwursts are pre-cooked during the simmering stage, so grilling merely adds smoke flavor and provides a browned/grilled appearance.) After grilling, hold brats in warmed beer and onion mixture, but do not allow sauce to boil. Serve with rolls/buns and desired condiments.

Tips for grilling brats: Flare-ups blacken the brats, so treat them with care, avoiding punctures and squeezing too hard. If flare-ups develop, move brats as far from flames as possible and immediately close the grill cover and vents for a short time. Alternately, a spray bottle of water can be used to douse flare-ups.

German Potato Salad

Makes 8 to 10 servings

Ingredients

12 to 14 (about 4 lbs.) medium red potatoes*, cooked, peeled and sliced
2 hard-boiled eggs, sliced
4 slices bacon, diced
1 medium onion, chopped
2 C. water
½ C. vinegar
½ C. sugar
2 T. cornstarch
4 tsp. salt
1½ tsp. prepared brown mustard
1 tsp. celery salt
¼ tsp. ground black pepper

Instructions

In a large bowl, combine potatoes and eggs; set aside. In a large skillet over medium to medium-high heat, cook bacon and onion until bacon is lightly crisp and onion is translucent. Drain, reserving 3 tablespoons drippings. Add bacon and onion to potato mixture. In the skillet, add remaining ingredients to drippings and cook over medium to medium-high heat until slightly thickened. Pour over potato mixture and toss to coat. Serve warm.

*Red potatoes will remain firm even when cooked, so they won't break apart when tossed.

Fresh Orchard Apple Crisp

Beautiful apple orchards grace rural Wisconsin, especially near the town of Gays Mills in the Kickapoo Valley. The orchards are a favorite local tourist spot throughout the fall, attracting apple lovers from neighboring states as well.

Makes 12 servings

Ingredients

1 C. sugar
1 tsp. ground cinnamon
1 C. plus 3 T. flour, divided
12 C. peeled and sliced baking apples*
1 C. margarine or butter, melted
1½ C. quick oats
1 C. brown sugar
Vanilla ice cream, optional

Instructions

Preheat oven to 350°F. In a medium bowl, combine sugar, cinnamon and 3 tablespoons flour. In a 9 x 13″ baking dish, spread apple slices as the bottom layer, then sprinkle sugar mixture evenly over apples; set aside. In a large bowl, stir together margarine, quick oats, brown sugar, and remaining 1 cup flour until well combined, creating a crumble mixture. Sprinkle crumble mixture over apples. Bake for 45 to 60 minutes or until apples feel soft when tested with a fork. If desired, serve warm or reheated with vanilla ice cream.

A few favorite baking apples include Jonathan, Fuji, Granny Smith, Rome Beauty and Pippin varieties.

Spiced Apple Cider

Makes 16 servings

Ingredients

1 gal. apple cider
1½ C. orange juice
½ C. brown sugar
6 cinnamon sticks
12 whole cloves
12 whole allspice

Instructions

In a large pot over high heat, combine all ingredients and bring to a boil. Reduce heat and simmer for a minimum of 30 minutes. Ladle from the top of the pot to serve, as spices will sink to the bottom.

Food for Thought

- Known as "America's Dairyland," Wisconsin's 1.3 million dairy cows make it the largest producer of cheese in the nation. The state produces more than 350 varieties of cheese.

- Wisconsin is also the nation's leading cranberry producer, accounting for nearly half of the country's total crop.

- Wisconsin has plentiful rivers and lakes, making it a great place to enjoy the fresh catch of the day. Favorites include walleye, perch, bluegills, trout and salmon.

- Many ethnic traditions are displayed in the special foods of Wisconsin. Danes make kringle, a special filled pastry; Belgians prepare booyah, a thick chicken and beef stew; Bavarians bake authentic pretzels that are dipped in mustard; Swedes fix Swedish pancakes; Germans make potato pancakes; and the list goes on and on...

While in the Area

- Watch a Green Bay Packer football game at a local restaurant near Lambeau stadium, because you probably won't be able to get tickets. The season-ticket waiting list for home games is about 80,000 people deep. The popular team received its moniker from the meat packing industry, as the Indian Packing Co. first supplied the team with uniforms and equipment back in 1919.

- Pick up Highway 51, just west of Pulaski, to enjoy a taste of rural Wisconsin. The scenic highway starts at the top of Wisconsin and ends just short of Louisiana's gulf coast. See animals or classic country barns and stop in to visit artists' studios, eat at little supper clubs or stay in a quaint bed and breakfast, as you travel through Wisconsin.

- Stop in the community of Tomahawk when you are traveling on Highway 51, where you can tour a Harley Davidson manufacturing facility. If you come on the right September day, you may witness the Fall Ride, when more than 40,000 bikers come to town.

Des Moines, Iowa
A Blue Ribbon Day

Family Party – Lunch for Eight
Dill Pickle-on-a-Stick
Deviled Egg-on-a-Stick
Fruit-on-a-Stick & Easy Sweet Dip
Hot Beef Sundae
Corn on the Cob-on-a-Stick
Caramel Apples-on-a-Stick
Funnel Cakes

About your Destination

"Is this Heaven?" "No, it's Iowa," is the famous movie line that describes the state perfectly. In the heartland of America, Iowa is waiting to welcome you with small town charm. Miles of lush green fields stretch under the summer sun to produce a plentiful harvest of golden corn and soybeans in the fall. The quilt-like pattern of planted fields is sprinkled with fertile creek-lined pastures for grazing cattle.

Iowa's deep agricultural roots are witnessed with a trip to the Iowa State Fair, held in one of Iowa's modern cities, Des Moines. The internationally-acclaimed fair, held over ten hot August days, is the single largest event in the State of Iowa, attracting more than a million people from all over the world. It is an

continued

Dill Pickle-on-a-Stick

Makes 8 servings

Ingredients

8 medium to large whole dill pickles,
   drained
8 (5″ to 7″) wood or bamboo skewers

Instructions

Skewer each whole pickle through one
end and slide it onto skewer until secure.
Tray and serve.

Deviled Egg-on-a-Stick

Makes 8 servings

Ingredients

2 tsp. dry ranch dressing mix
2 T. sugar
1 T. dried minced onions
¼ tsp. garlic powder
1 tsp. prepared horseradish
1 T. prepared yellow mustard
¼ C. lite sour cream
¼ C. mayonnaise
8 hard-boiled eggs, peeled and chilled
8 (5″ to 7″) wood or bamboo skewers
   or pretzel sticks

Instructions

In a medium bowl, combine first
8 ingredients; stir until well blended.
Refrigerate for 2 to 12 hours to allow
flavors to blend. Skewer whole hard-
boiled eggs onto skewers or pretzel sticks
and serve with prepared sauce on the side.

Note: *This sauce is also excellent served
with pretzels.*

continued from page 32
outstanding agricultural
showplace, boasting one of
the world's largest livestock
shows. The Fair also provides
spectacular entertainment,
a midway, arts and crafts
exhibits, horticultural
displays, incredible foods,
and so much more. The Iowa
State Fair has evolved from
a simple stock show to an
entertainment extravaganza,
but it has never strayed from
its focus of celebrating blue
ribbon excellence.

Theme & Setting

Gather for "A Blue Ribbon
Day" while enjoying food
on a stick. Each year more
and more foods are served
on-a-stick at the State Fair.
Some of the favorites are
pork chop-on-a-stick, deep-
fried candy bar-on-a-stick
and monkey tail, a chocolate
covered banana-on-a-stick.
After a Hot Beef Sundae
and some Corn on the Cob,
play some games at your
homemade "midway" before
eating up funnel cakes
dusted with powdered sugar.
Set up simple games like
ring-toss or knock-down-pop-
bottles-with-baseballs, or have
a talent show with blue ribbon
awards. Face painting will
make little ones feel like they
are at the Fair. Decorations
of colored bunting, balloons
and blue ribbons will add a
finishing touch to your setting.

Fruit-on-a-Stick & Easy Sweet Dip

Makes 8 servings

Ingredients

1 (8 oz.) container frozen whipped topping, thawed

1 C. yogurt, any flavor

1 C. large seedless grapes

1 C. whole strawberries, stemmed

1 C. apple chunks, 1″ pieces

1 C. pineapple chunks, 1″ pieces

16 (7″ to 9″) wood or bamboo skewers

Instructions

In a medium bowl, blend whipped topping and yogurt. Cover and chill for 30 minutes. Thread fruit onto skewers in random patterns. Serve with Easy Sweet Dip on the side.

Hot Beef Sundae

A relatively new tradition at the Iowa State Fair is the Hot Beef Sundae. The hot beef sandwich is a traditional comfort–food dish served across the states, especially in the Midwest. But this silly version, served in a bowl, is sure to bring a smile to a kid of any age.

Makes 8 servings

Ingredients for beef & gravy

2 (10.5 oz.) cans cream of mushroom soup

⅓ C. sherry wine, cooking wine or water

1 (1 to 1.25 oz.) env. onion soup mix

3 lbs. boneless chuck roast

1 (.75 to .87 oz.) env. brown gravy mix

½ C. water

Ingredients for mashed potatoes

3 lbs. Yukon gold potatoes, peeled and quartered

1 tsp. salt

½ C. heavy whipping cream

¼ C. butter

2 T. milk

Salt and pepper to taste

Iowa Quick Facts

Date of Statehood:	December 28, 1846
Population:	2,926,324
Capital:	Des Moines
State Bird:	Eastern Goldfinch
State Flower:	Wild Prairie Rose
State Nickname:	Hawkeye State

OUR LIBERTIES WE PRIZE AND OUR RIGHTS WE WILL MAINTAIN

IOWA

Ingredients for sundae

Beef and gravy
Mashed potatoes
2 C. shredded Cheddar cheese
8 cherry tomatoes

Instructions

To make beef and gravy: In a medium to large bowl, combine mushroom soup, wine or water and onion soup mix. Place roast in a slow cooker; pour soup mixture over roast. Cover and cook on low for 2 hours. In a small bowl, whisk brown gravy mix with water, add mixture to the cooking roast. Cook roast for an additional 3 to 4 hours or until meat is tender. Transfer meat to cutting board and shred or cut into serving pieces; return to gravy mixture. *To make mashed potatoes:* Place potatoes and 1 teaspoon salt in a large saucepan and add enough water to just cover the potatoes. Bring to a boil, then reduce heat and simmer while covered for 15 to 20 minutes or until tender. In a microwave or saucepan, heat cream and butter until butter is melted. Drain water from potatoes. In a large bowl, combine potatoes and warm cream mixture. With a potato masher, mash potatoes until smooth. Stir in extra milk to reach desired consistency and add salt and pepper to taste.

To assemble sundaes: Scoop mashed potatoes into large individual bowls. Spoon beef and gravy over mashed potatoes. Top mixture with some shredded cheese and a cherry tomato. Serve with spoons (and forks) as you would a sundae.

Corn on the Cob-on-a-Stick

Makes 8 servings

Ingredients

8 (7″ to 9″) heavy-duty skewers
8 ears fresh sweet corn, husked and cleaned
1 stick butter
Salt and pepper to taste

Instructions

Insert a skewer into the wide end of each cob of corn. In a medium to large stock pot, place ears of corn on end, skewers upward. Add enough water to cover corn; bring to a boil over medium-high heat. Boil 4 to 8 minutes to desired tenderness. Place butter on a plate and roll corn in butter. Serve warm with salt and pepper to individual taste.

Caramel Apples-on-a-Stick

Makes 8 servings

Ingredients

8 medium tart apples
8 wooden sticks
1 C. butter
2 C. brown sugar
1 C. light corn syrup
1 (14 oz.) can sweetened
 condensed milk
2 tsp. vanilla extract
Candies or nuts, optional
Butter or nonstick cooking spray

Instructions

Wash and dry apples, rubbing off any wax coating. Remove the stems. Insert a wooden stick into each apple. In a heavy saucepan, combine butter, brown sugar, corn syrup and milk; bring to a boil over medium-high heat. While continuously stirring, cook on low for 30 to 40 minutes until candy thermometer reaches 248°F (firm ball stage). Remove from heat and stir in vanilla. Dip each apple into hot caramel mixture and turn to coat. If desired, sprinkle with candies or nuts. Set on generously buttered or sprayed waxed or parchment paper to cool.

Funnel Cakes

Makes 8 servings

Ingredients

3 C. vegetable oil
4 C. flour
⅓ C. sugar
2 tsp. baking powder
½ tsp. salt
2½ C. milk
3 large eggs
Powdered sugar for dusting
Special equipment – deep-frying
 thermometer

Instructions

In a deep medium skillet or deep-fat fryer, heat oil over medium-high heat until it reaches 350° to 375°F. Meanwhile, in a large bowl, whisk together flour, sugar, baking powder and salt. Add milk and eggs; whisk until smooth. Place batter in a large resealable bag, remove excess air and seal shut. Using a scissors, cut off one bottom corner of the bag, making a ¼″-wide hole. Carefully squeeze about 1 cup of batter back and forth into the oil in a freeform pattern. Set the bag aside in a bowl, with the slit side up, to prevent spills and drips between batches. Fry for about 2 minutes, until golden on the bottom. Using tongs, turn funnel cake over and cook for about 1 more minute, until second side is golden. Remove from oil and drain on paper towel-lined plate. Repeat with remaining batter. Dust cakes with powdered sugar; serve hot.

Food for Thought

- Iowa is the number one corn-producing state in the U.S. Much of the corn grown in Iowa is used to feed cattle, hogs, sheep and poultry, indirectly providing meat, dairy and eggs as well. The rest is used in processed food, such as corn syrup and cereal, or for plastics and renewable energy. This corn is not a garden variety, but rather, it is a hard grain. Ask an Iowan, however, and you will find out that the best garden sweet corn for eating corn-on-the-cob also grows in Iowa.

- Family-owned farms still make up the large majority of Iowa farms, where conservation practices, diversity of crops and preserving the rural way of life is very important. Some of the diverse crops sold at farmers markets include apples, strawberries, grapes, sweet corn and popcorn.

- Coalitions of farmers have been formed to further agricultural industries of the state, such as the Iowa Egg Council, the Iowa Corn Growers Association and the Iowa Pork Producers. Their product development and marketing promote agricultural products and educate the population. An example of product development is the "Iowa Chop," a thickly cut pork chop from the marbled section of the center cut loin; it's great on the grill.

While in the Area

- See the famous Butter Cow while you attend the Iowa State Fair. A butter sculpture of a cow has been a feature of the Iowa State Fair since the early 1900s, and although a real dairy cow weighs more than 1,000 pounds, 600 pounds of sweet cream Iowa butter are used to create a likeness each year.

- Drive the country roads southwest of Des Moines to cross the creeks by way of the historic covered bridges of Madison County. Six of the county's original 19 bridges remain today, all of which are listed on the National Register of Historic Places. The original bridges of Madison County date back to the 1800s.

- Sit down at a family dinner in the Amana Colonies to the east of Des Moines. The seven colonies represent the communal life they were once founded upon. With a German heritage, original commune members hoped to find religious freedom as they traveled to the new land. After arriving in Iowa, they settled into their communal life, which lasted until the 1930s when it was set aside in order to preserve their communities and prevent their children from leaving. Today the Colonies attract hundreds of thousands of visitors each year with the charm of historic brick streets, stone and clapboard homes and restaurants, as well as shops and woolen mills.

Kansas City, Missouri
BBQ and All That Jazz

Dinner for Four to Eight
Great American Macaroni Salad
K.C. BBQ Ribs
Classic Cream Corn Bake
Jazzed-Up BBQ Beans
Buttermilk Brownies

About your Destination

The history of the United States may not be long, but it is rich. Missouri and Kansas City are great examples of the important roles the Midwest played in American history. The movement westward for thousands who traveled the difficult Oregon and California Trails began in the then-frontier Missouri towns of Independence and Westport. (Both are now part of Kansas City.) The Santa Fe Trail, which also began in Missouri, was a two-way commercial route with a primary purpose of profit, as opposed to the mostly one-way Oregon and California Trails traveled for the sake of homesteading. The history of these trails is the focus of the Frontier Trails Center and a highlight of the Kansas City Museum, and other small monuments and historic trail sites.

continued

Great American Macaroni Salad

continued from page 38

Makes 8 servings

Ingredients for salad

8 oz. cellentani* noodles, cooked according to package directions
1 C. diced green bell pepper
¾ C. diced celery
½ C. diced cucumbers, seeded
⅓ C. chopped green olives
⅓ C. sliced black olives
¼ C. thinly sliced red onion
3 T. pimento
4 oz. sharp Cheddar cheese, diced
¼ C. chopped fresh parsley

Ingredients for dressing

½ C. mayonnaise
¼ C. sour cream
1 T. white wine vinegar
1 tsp. crushed garlic
½ tsp. ground mustard
¼ tsp. salt
¼ tsp. ground black pepper
¼ tsp. paprika
¼ tsp. hot pepper sauce

Instructions

In a large bowl, combine rinsed and cooled noodles with remaining salad ingredients and set aside. In a medium bowl, whisk together dressing ingredients until well blended. Pour dressing over salad ingredients and stir until evenly combined. Cover and refrigerate for 4 to 24 hours. Stir well before serving.

Cellantani is a hollow spiral-shaped noodle. Replace cellantini with gemelli, campanelle or other pasta noodles if necessary.

A review of more recent years in Kansas City's past reveals a literal taste of American history... barbecue! The Carolinas boast the beginnings of American barbecue, and Texas is the brisket capital of the world, but Kansas City brought it all together, becoming famous for BBQ and home to more than 90 barbecue joints. It began in the early 1900s in an old trolley barn at 19th and Highland. The tradition has carried on with dry rubbed, slow roasted barbecue over a pit of hickory and slathered with smooth, rich, sweetly tangy sauce.

Theme & Setting

You can't really think of Kansas City barbecue without thinking of jazz. Some of the greatest jazz players started in the clubs of Kansas City and gave the town a sound of its own, described as a blues-based, swing style jazz. And while New Orleans was the birthplace of jazz, America's music grew up in Kansas City. Live music was heard all over the city, in hotels, clubs, casinos and music halls. Today's Jazz is alive and well in Kansas City where you can hear the music or explore the history.

Create your own jazz club setting with dim lighting and intimate seating. Black tablecloths and a glowing candle centerpiece create club ambiance. Use funky jazz glassware and coasters representing the 1920s and 1930s. Add the sparkle of white twinkle lights draped in the room. Of course, welcome guests with the classic sounds and smells of Kansas City as you prepare to serve up BBQ and All That Jazz!

K.C. BBQ Ribs

Makes 4 large or 8 small servings

Ingredients for rub

1 C. brown sugar
2 T. paprika
2 tsp. ground black pepper
2 tsp. chili powder
2 tsp. onion powder
1 tsp. garlic powder
1 tsp. ground mustard
½ tsp. cayenne pepper

Ingredients for ribs

2 slabs pork spare ribs,
    3 lbs. each

Ingredients for sauce

3 C. water
1 C. ketchup
⅔ C. cider vinegar
½ C. tomato paste
½ C. molasses
¼ C. sugar
1 T. liquid smoke flavoring*
1 tsp. onion powder
1 tsp. black pepper
1 tsp. Worcestershire sauce
¼ tsp. garlic powder

Instructions

Before preparing the rub, spread brown sugar on a baking sheet to dry for 2 to 24 hours. When sugar is dry, combine all rub ingredients; set aside. Remove the thick membrane covering the bone side of each slab of ribs. Massage the rub into the ribs, wrap in plastic and refrigerate for 1 hour or up to overnight. To prepare barbecue sauce, in a large saucepan over medium-high heat, stir together sauce ingredients and bring to a boil. Reduce heat to medium and continue to simmer, stirring often, for 30 minutes or until barbecue sauce thickens. Use immediately or chill overnight for best flavor. Reserve some sauce for serving. Cook ribs as directed below; remove from grill or oven and allow to stand for about 10 minutes. (Discard sauce that has been exposed to basting utensils/ raw meat.) To serve, cut slabs into individual ribs and serve hot with reserved BBQ sauce on the side.

If cooking ribs on the grill: Place ribs meat-side down next to medium-hot coals that are about 225°F; cover grill. The indirect heat will cook them slower, making them tender; adjust grill vents to maintain an even temperature. Allow to cook for 1 hour, then baste with barbecue sauce and continue to cook for 3 to 4 hours, turning and basting every half hour until tender.

If baking ribs in the oven: Preheat oven to 350°F. Place ribs in a roasting pan with a rack. Heavily baste ribs with sauce and tent a piece of aluminum foil over top. Bake for 2½ to 3 hours or until fork-tender, basting every thirty minutes; remove foil for last 30 minutes.

Note on smoking: *Hardwoods can be added to grills and special smoker bags with wood chip flavorings are available for use with grills or ovens. These products help to produce a smokier taste. Follow manufacturer's instructions.*

Liquid Smoke is a bottled liquid made by capturing and condensing the vapors from burning wet wood chips. Find it displayed near barbecue sauces in the supermarket.

Classic Cream Corn Bake

Makes 4 to 6 servings

Ingredients

1 (15.2 oz.) can whole kernel corn, drained
1 (14.7 oz.) can cream-style corn
1 (8.5 oz.) pkg. corn muffin mix (such as Jiffy brand)
1 C. sour cream
½ C. butter, melted
1½ C. shredded Cheddar cheese

Instructions

Preheat oven to 350°F. In a large bowl, stir together whole kernel corn, creamed corn, corn muffin mix, sour cream and melted butter. Pour into a greased 9 x 13″ baking dish and bake for 45 minutes or until golden brown. Remove from oven and sprinkle with cheese. Return dish to oven for 5 to 10 minutes or until cheese is melted. Let stand for a minimum of 5 minutes and serve warm.

Jazzed-Up BBQ Beans

Makes 4 to 6 servings

Ingredients

1 (28 oz.) can pork & beans
1 C. chopped brisket*
1 C. barbecue sauce
¼ C. brown sugar
1 T. chili powder
1 tsp. liquid smoke flavoring
½ C. ketchup
½ C. water

Instructions

In a stock pot, stir together all ingredients. Over medium heat, bring beans to a boil; reduce heat to simmer. Cook for 20 minutes or until a thick, soupy consistency is reached. Alternatively, cook in a grill-safe baking pan on the grill. Serve hot.

Packaged, prepared chopped brisket or roast pieces are available in the deli case of most supermarkets.

Missouri Quick Facts

Date of Statehood:	August 10, 1821
Population:	5,595,211
Capital:	Jefferson City
State Bird:	Bluebird
State Flower:	Hawthorn
State Nickname:	Show Me State

Buttermilk Brownies

Makes 24 brownies

Ingredients for brownies
2 C. flour
2 C. sugar
1 tsp. baking soda
¼ tsp. salt
1 C. butter
⅓ C. unsweetened cocoa powder
1 C. water
2 large eggs
½ C. buttermilk
1½ tsp. vanilla extract

Ingredients for frosting
¼ C. butter
3 T. unsweetened cocoa powder
3 T. buttermilk
2¼ C. sifted powdered sugar
½ tsp. vanilla extract

Instructions
Preheat oven to 350°F. Grease a 10 x 15″ or a 9 x 13″ baking pan; set aside. In a large mixing bowl, combine flour, sugar, baking soda and salt; set aside. In a medium saucepan, combine butter, cocoa powder and water. Bring mixture just to boiling while stirring constantly. Remove from heat and add chocolate mixture to flour mixture; beat on medium speed until combined. Add eggs, buttermilk and vanilla; continue to beat for 1 minute (batter will be thin). Pour batter into prepared pan. Bake for 25 to 35 minutes or until a wooden toothpick inserted in the center comes out clean; set aside on wire rack. To make frosting while brownies are just beginning to cool, in a medium saucepan, combine butter, cocoa powder and buttermilk. Over medium-high heat, bring mixture to a boil; remove from heat and beat in powdered sugar and vanilla until smooth. Pour warm frosting over warm brownies, spreading evenly. Continue to cool brownies on wire rack. Cut to serve.

Food for Thought

- Plain ol' steak, not just BBQ, is popular in Kansas City as well. Located in the heartland, beef is fresh and readily available.

- Missouri is the largest producer of black walnuts in the world, producing 50% of the international crop per year. Pecans and hickory nuts are also a sizeable crop for Missouri.

- Honey, another product of the state, became the source of a famous historical disagreement regarding the location of the boundary line between Missouri and Iowa. The dispute became known as the Honey War.

While in the Area

- Enjoy the beautiful water fountains of Kansas City, said to be home to more fountains than any other city in the world, except Rome. The craftsmanship and presentation is as impressive as the quantity of fountains.

- Shop the stores of Country Club Plaza, where you can enjoy some of the most famous Kansas City fountains. The Plaza attracts millions of tourists each year who enjoy not only the shops, fountains and outdoor dining, but also the architecture and special holiday lighting.

- Go downtown to Fifth and Walnut, just off the banks of the Missouri River to find the historic City Market. The area was originally known as the Town of Kansas and was lively in the mid-1800s, with saloons and bars running along Main Street. Today, the lively outdoor venue hosts farmers markets, Sunday art fairs, the Arabia Steamboat Museum, and numerous jazz and BBQ events.

Louisville, Kentucky
Run for the Roses Breakfast

Breakfast for Four
Cheese Grits
Country Scrambled Eggs
Maple-Glazed Breakfast Ham
Cinnamon Raisin Biscuits
Slow-Cooked Apple Butter
Good Mornin' Orange Juice

Another Taste of Kentucky
Mint Julep

About your Destination

Horse racing in Kentucky began its rich history in the late 1700s when men began racing in a park-like block in the town of Lexington. After a couple of years, safety complaints led to the organization of a Jockey Club. Different tracks were popular over the first 100 years of racing in Kentucky, but in 1875, Churchill Downs became the home of the famous Kentucky Derby. The twin spires atop the homestretch of the grandstands were added in 1895 and remain one of the most recognized structures in all of sports. The Kentucky Derby is an annual "Run for the Roses" and the first leg of the United States Triple Crown of thoroughbred horse racing. Roses were

continued

Cheese Grits

Makes 4 servings

Ingredients

2 C. whole milk
2 C. water
1½ tsp. salt
1 C. coarsely ground cornmeal
½ tsp. ground black pepper
¼ C.unsalted butter
¾ C. shredded sharp
    Cheddar cheese

Instructions

In a large heavy pot, bring milk, water and salt to a boil over medium-high heat. Once it has reached boiling, gradually add cornmeal while whisking constantly. When all cornmeal is incorporated, decrease heat to low and cover. Remove lid and whisk frequently, every 3 to 4 minutes, to prevent lumps from forming and grits from sticking to the pan. Cook for 20 to 25 minutes or until mixture is creamy. Remove from heat, and whisk in pepper and butter. When butter has melted, gradually whisk in cheese. Serve immediately.

continued from page 44

first established as part of the Derby celebration when they were presented to all the ladies in attendance. They were such a hit that the president of Churchill Downs at that time adopted the rose as the race's official flower. Each year, a garland of 554 roses is presented to the winner.

Theme & Setting

The Run for the Roses Breakfast menu has been planned in the fashion of the original Derby Breakfast served at the Governor's Mansion in 1936. The tradition of breakfast on race day began when Governor A.B. "Happy" Chandler invited a few friends to a small and informal, yet elegant meal before the 62nd running of the Kentucky Derby. Without knowing it, he began a tradition that continues today, but has grown considerably in size. Today, over 10,000 guests gather on the Capitol grounds to participate in this annual breakfast with singing, dancing, storytelling, face-painting, theatrical performances and more.

The race day breakfast tradition is also celebrated in many Southern homes, as Kentuckians and their guests sit down to private versions of the Governor's feast. Celebrate Southern hospitality on a day of your choosing when you host a Run for the Roses breakfast for your family or friends. A centerpiece including roses would be an exceptional way to decorate within the theme, and if it does happen to be race day, refresh with a Mint Julep while you take in the most exciting two minutes in sports.

Country Scrambled Eggs

Makes 4 servings

Ingredients

6 large eggs
⅓ C. milk
Salt and pepper to taste
1 T. butter
1 medium tomato, chopped
1 T. chopped green onion tops
  or chives

Instructions

In a large bowl, beat eggs. Add milk and whisk together. Blend in salt and pepper to taste. In a large skillet, melt butter over medium-low heat. Pour egg mixture into skillet. Gently stir eggs with a spatula or wooden spoon, to scramble while cooking. Just as eggs are no longer liquid, fold in tomato and green onion. Heat through and serve immediately, while eggs still retain a moist appearance.

Maple-Glazed Breakfast Ham

Makes 4 servings

Ingredients

¼ C. maple syrup
1 T. apple cider vinegar
1 T. Dijon mustard
1 (1¼ lb.) ham steak

Instructions

In a small bowl, combine maple syrup, vinegar and mustard. Brush one side of ham steak with syrup mixture and place glazed side down in a large skillet. Brush remainder of syrup mixture on the top of ham. Cook over medium heat, turning frequently, until cooked through and glaze has thickened.

Kentucky Quick Facts

Date of Statehood:	June 1, 1792
Population:	4,041,769
Capital:	Frankfort
State Bird:	Cardinal
State Flower:	Goldenrod
State Nickname:	Bluegrass State

Cinnamon Raisin Biscuits

Makes 12 biscuits

Ingredients

2 C. self-rising flour
1 tsp. baking powder
¼ tsp. salt
1 tsp. baking soda
¼ C. sugar
¼ C. plus 2 T. shortening
¾ C. buttermilk
½ C. raisins
1½ tsp. ground cinnamon
Flour for working the dough
1 C. powdered sugar
⅛ tsp. vanilla extract
2 T. milk, plus additional for
  consistency

Instructions

In a large mixing bowl, combine first five ingredients. Cut in shortening with a fork or pastry blender until mixture is crumbly. Add buttermilk and stir until just blended. Fold in raisins and cinnamon; do not mix batter more than necessary. Preheat oven to 400°F. Scrape dough onto a well-floured work surface; sprinkle top of dough with flour and pat down with hands to ½″ thickness. Cut with 2″ round cutter and place on a greased baking sheet. Bake for 10 to 15 minutes or until golden brown. Meanwhile, in a small bowl, combine powdered sugar, vanilla and milk to make icing. Stir in additional milk, 1 teaspoon at a time, until icing reaches desired consistency. Drizzle icing over warm biscuits to serve.

Slow-Cooked Apple Butter

Makes 6 cups

Ingredients

4 lbs. cooking apples, peeled
  and sliced
½ C. apple cider vinegar
3 C. sugar
1 C. brown sugar
½ tsp. ground nutmeg
1 T. ground cinnamon
¼ tsp. ground cloves

Instructions

In a 4-quart slow cooker, combine apples and vinegar. Cover and cook on high for 6 hours. Stir in sugars and spices, reduce heat to low, cover and cook for 4 hours. Serve warm, or cool and refrigerate for up to 1 week.

Good Mornin' Orange Juice

Makes 4 servings

Ingredients

1 (6 oz.) can frozen orange juice
 concentrate, thawed
⅓ C. sugar
⅓ C. instant nonfat dry milk powder
2 tsp. vanilla extract
¾ C. cold water
10 to 12 ice cubes
Orange slices, optional

Instructions

Combine orange juice, sugar, milk
powder, vanilla and water in a
blender; cover and blend on high
speed. Add ice cubes, a few at a
time, processing until slushy. If
desired, garnish the edge of each
glass with an orange slice and serve.

Mint Julep

Makes 10 to 12 servings

Ingredients

40 small fresh spearmint leaves
4 C. bourbon
1 C. sugar
1 C. distilled water
Shaved ice
Mint sprigs for garnish
Drinking straws
Powdered sugar, optional

Instructions

Place washed mint leaves in a
medium bowl; cover with 3 ounces
bourbon and soak for 15 minutes.
Carefully gather leaves in a paper
towel and wring the liquid from
the mint into the bowl. Place
leaves back in the bourbon bowl;
repeat wringing and soaking
process several more times. Discard
wrung-out leaves and towels; set
minted bourbon aside. In a small
saucepan, stir sugar and water over
low heat until dissolved; set aside
to cool. In a large glass pitcher, stir
together remaining bourbon and
cooled sugar syrup. Add minted
bourbon, 1 tablespoon at a time, to
desired taste. Chill for a minimum
of 24 hours. To serve, fill each glass
(or silver mint julep cup) half full
with shaved ice, insert mint sprig,
short straw and more shaved ice
to almost full. When frost has
formed on the surface of the cup,
pour julep over ice and, if desired,
sprinkle powdered sugar on top.
Serve immediately.

Food for Thought

- String beans have deep roots in Kentucky. Efforts have been made in recent years throughout Kentucky to preserve heirloom varieties of beans. Their appearance varies widely: long and short, stout and stringy, purple or speckled. Names are sometimes assigned to the beans based on the name of the family that grew them. Some estimates indicate that over a thousand varieties are grown throughout Appalachia.

- The paw paw tree is a Kentucky native producing fruit that is exotic and delicious, almost tropical in taste. Because it ripens very quickly, the harvest only lasts a few days, and because the fruit bruises easily, it does not remain fresh for long.

- Chess pies are a Southern specialty with some variation, but generally include a single crust with a simple filling of eggs, sugar, butter and a small amount of flour. The pie is very sweet and it's often enjoyed with a cup of coffee in order to offset the sweetness.

While in the Area

- Swing a Louisville Slugger™. Louisville, Kentucky is the home of the most popular baseball bat brand in history, the Louisville Slugger™. Over 100,000,000 bats have been sold by this company, which began more then 120 years ago as a wood shop that turned out butter churns.

- Take a scenic drive along the Kentucky Bourbon Trail. Kentucky is famous for its bourbon. Early settlers included many Scotch and Irish immigrants who brought their whiskey-making skills to America. Corn was used to make this new style of whiskey that is aged in charred barrels. Today, more than 95% of the world's bourbon is distilled and aged in Kentucky. That's because Kentucky has the perfect mix of climate and resources. Tour distilleries on the Kentucky Bourbon Trail to learn about the history and heritage of bourbon.

- See the London's Royal Armouries display at the Frazier Museum in Louisville. The Frazier Museum is a cultural arts institution dedicated to telling the complete American story, including British and European roots.

Williamsburg, Virginia
The 12th Night Colonial Celebration

Four Course Dinner for Eight
Winter Wassail
Peanut Soup
Virginia Crab Salad
Spoon Bread
Spiced Apple Pork Roast
Creamed Pearl Onions
Orange King's Cake

About your Destination

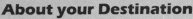

Colonial Williamsburg gained strength and size after the Statehouse in Jamestown (the first English settlement) burned for the fourth time in 1698. For most of the 18th century, Williamsburg was the center of government, education and culture in the Colony of Virginia, where Thomas Jefferson, Patrick Henry, James Monroe, James Madison and others worked together to shape the beginnings of our great democracy.

Today, Colonial Williamsburg is the nation's largest living history museum, encompassing around 300 acres, including 500 buildings, homes, stores and taverns that have been reconstructed and restored to their 1700s appearance. The daily life of colonists, including many enslaved and free black Americans, is

continued

Winter Wassail

Once a simple greeting, the term wassail is now used as both a verb and a noun. The verb is "toasting," and the noun is a "beverage" or punch served from a bowl. The old English word is part of the traditional Christmas carol that starts with, "Here we come a wassailing…"

<u>*Makes 20 servings*</u>

Ingredients

1 gal. apple cider
1 (46 oz.) can unsweetened pineapple juice
¾ C. brewed tea
1 T. whole cloves
1 T. whole allspice
2 cinnamon sticks

Instructions

In a large stock pot or electric slow cooker, combine liquid ingredients. Place cloves, allspice and cinnamon sticks in a cheesecloth sack or a tea ball strainer and add to liquid ingredients. Over low heat, simmer for 4 to 6 hours. Add water if it evaporates too much. Serve warm.

continued from page 50
presented through reenactments. A visit will bring the history of the U.S.A. alive as the beginnings of our country, and the role Williamsburg played in the events leading up to the Revolutionary War, are highlighted.

Theme & Setting

Twelfth Night, as celebrated in 18th century cities like Williamsburg, was a high-spirited mid-winter event whose practices date back to ancient Rome. The twelfth and final night of the Christmas season is celebrated on January 5th (or 6th in some places) with final frenzy of feasting and merry-making. Like the European custom, it marks the end of the holiday season before the community returns to the daily grind of winter.

Send handwritten invitations on parchment penned with old English language and charm. After guests arrive, toast with Winter Wassail served from sturdy mugs or metal steins. Wooden bowls and spoons and rustic cloth napkins will add to the Old-World feel, while you dine, as dripping taper candles provide light and ambiance. Fill the night with singing, dancing and storytelling; then finish the evening by reading the proclamation of pronouncements and predictions for the New Year.

Peanut Soup

Makes 8 to 10 servings

Ingredients

6 C. chicken broth
2 C. creamy peanut butter
¼ tsp. celery salt
¼ tsp. onion salt
2 tsp. sugar
2⅔ C. half & half
Chopped peanuts for topping
Sour cream, optional

Instructions

In a large stock pot, heat broth to boiling. Reduce heat to medium and add peanut butter; stir until very smooth. Add celery salt and onion salt. Stir in sugar and half & half. Heat through, but do not boil. Top with chopped peanuts and, if desired, a small dollop of sour cream.

Virginia Crab Salad

Makes 8 servings

Ingredients

2 lbs. cooked or imitation crabmeat
2 C. diced celery
⅔ C. mayonnaise
2 T. lemon juice
1 tsp. salt
Dash of white pepper
⅛ tsp. hot pepper sauce
½ tsp. Worcestershire sauce
¼ C. Italian dressing
Lettuce leaves as garnish

Instructions

Discard any bits of shell or cartilage if using real crabmeat, or break imitation crabmeat into smaller pieces. In a large bowl, combine crabmeat and celery; set aside. In a medium bowl, combine mayonnaise, lemon juice, salt, pepper, sauces and dressing; mix well. Fold dressing into crab and celery mixture. Chill. Serve on lettuce leaf-lined plates.

Virginia Quick Facts

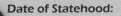

Date of Statehood:	June 25, 1788
Population:	7,078,515
Capital:	Richmond
State Bird:	Cardinal
State Flower:	Dogwood
State Nickname:	Old Dominion State

Spoon Bread

This pudding-like bread is soft enough to serve and eat with a spoon, making the original name "Spoon Bread," quite perfect.

Makes 6 to 8 servings

Ingredients

1½ C. cornmeal
¼ tsp. salt
1 T. sugar
1½ C. boiling water
2 T. butter, melted
1½ C. milk
4 large eggs, well beaten
1 T. baking powder

Instructions

Preheat oven to 375°F. In a large mixing bowl, combine cornmeal, salt and sugar. With an electric mixer on low speed, blend in boiling water and butter; mix for 5 minutes. Add milk and beaten eggs; mix for an additional 5 minutes. Allow mixture to stand for 5 minutes to cool. Turn mixer on low and blend in baking powder until fully incorporated. Pour mixture into a buttered skillet or 2-quart casserole and bake for 30 to 45 minutes, until center has set. Serve immediately.

Spiced Apple Pork Roast

Makes 8 to 12 servings

Ingredients

1 C. applesauce
⅓ C. brown sugar
2 tsp. vinegar
⅛ to ¼ tsp. ground cloves
1 (3 to 4 lb.) boneless pork loin roast, trimmed
1 clove garlic, peeled and slivered
2 T. flour
1 tsp. salt
½ tsp. sugar
⅛ tsp. ground black pepper
1 tsp. prepared brown mustard

Instructions

Preheat oven to 350°F. In a small bowl, combine applesauce, brown sugar, vinegar and cloves; set aside. Cut slits in surface of roast and insert slivers of garlic. In a small bowl, combine flour, salt, sugar, pepper and mustard. Rub flour mixture over roast. Place roast on a rack in a shallow roasting pan. Bake uncovered for 30 minutes, then brush applesauce mixture over the roast. Bake uncovered for an additional 30 to 40 minutes, until meat thermometer reaches 160°F. Remove roast and allow to stand briefly; slice to serve.

Creamed Pearl Onions

Makes 8 to 10 servings

Ingredients

2 lbs. pearl onions, peeled
2 T. butter
2 T. flour
½ tsp. salt
¼ tsp. ground black pepper
1¼ C. half & half
¼ C. reserved water from cooking
onions
⅓ C. chopped dry roasted peanuts

Instructions

In a medium to large pot, boil
onions in water until just tender.
Drain onions, reserving ¼ cup
cooking water. Place onions in
a shallow baking dish and set
aside. Preheat oven to 350°F. In
a medium saucepan, melt butter
and blend in flour, salt and pepper.
Cook over low heat while stirring
constantly, for 2 minutes or until
smooth and bubbly. Stir in half
& half and reserved onion water
and return to a boil; continue to
boil for 1 minute. Pour hot cream
mixture over onions and sprinkle
with chopped peanuts. Bake for 15
minutes, then let stand for
5 to 10 minutes before serving.

Orange King's Cake

Makes 8 servings

Ingredients

2¼ C. flour
1 tsp. baking soda
½ tsp. salt
1 C. raisins
½ C. chopped walnuts
½ C. shortening
2 C. sugar, divided
2 large eggs, beaten
1 tsp. vanilla extract
1 T. orange zest
1 C. buttermilk
⅓ C. orange juice

Instructions

Preheat oven to 350°F. Sift
together flour, baking soda and
salt. Stir in raisins and nuts; set
aside. In a separate mixing bowl,
cream shortening and 1 cup sugar.
Beat in eggs, vanilla and orange
zest. Blend in flour mixture by
increments, alternating with
buttermilk. Pour batter into a
well greased 9˝ square pan or
Bundt pan. Bake for 40 minutes.
Meanwhile, combine orange juice
with remaining 1 cup sugar. Spread
orange juice mixture over hot cake.
Return cake to oven; bake for
10 minutes or until glaze bubbles
and a wooden toothpick inserted
in center of cake comes out clean.
Cool in pan before turning out
onto a serving plate.

Note: *To serve as a "king's cake," add
one large dry bean to the batter before
baking, or pass slips of marked paper
when serving dessert, to determine
the "king's identity."*

Food for Thought

- Historians research colonial dining habits, manners and customs in order to provide the most accurate replication possible. They have discovered that white tablecloths were changed after the first and second courses, but that the dessert course was served on the bare table.

- Multiculturalism influenced cuisine in the United States in its colonial days. The British, Africans, Native Americans and French each brought their heritage and ingredients to the "melting pot" and table of America.

- Regional favorites of Virginia include coastal crabs, oysters, clams and shrimp, as well as inland specialties like biscuits and gravy, spoon bread, country ham and red-eye gravy over grits.

While in the Area

- Visit historical Jamestown and Yorktown, the other cities which make up "America's Historic Triangle." Learn not only of the first settlements in America, but also about the Powhatans who first lived in Jamestown and the first major battle of the American Revolutionary War, fought in Yorktown.

- Step into the 1930s and 1940s as you enter Bassett Hall, a two-story 18th-century white frame farmhouse located on 585 acres of lawn, garden and woodlands. John D. Rockefeller, Jr. and his wife, Abby Aldrich Rockefeller, called Bassett Hall home during the time the restoration of Colonial Williamsburg had just began.

- Drive thirty minutes northwest of Williamsburg to visit Sherwood Forest Plantation, first recorded in a 1616 land grant and home of the 10th U.S. President, John Tyler. Tyler purchased the 1,600 acre property in 1842, when he renamed it "Sherwood Forest" to reference his reputation as a political outlaw. At 300 feet long, it is considered to be the longest frame house in America.

About the King's Cake

A Twelfth Night cake is sliced into enough pieces for each guest to have one. Whoever finds the bean which has been baked inside (or coin or cast metal version of Baby Jesus), is declared "king" for the evening. The king, sometimes referred to as the "Lord of Misrule," presides over the remainder of the evening's festivities.

Millen, Georgia
Meet Under the Old Magnolia

Picnic for Four to Six

Georgia Peach & Summer Fruit Salad
Corn Muffins with Honey Butter
Oven-Fried Picnic Chicken
Sweet Potato Salad
Pecan Pie Squares
Watermelon Lemonade

About your Destination

Magnolia Springs State Park lies five miles
north of Millen, Georgia, along Highway 25.
A beautiful boardwalk spans the waters which
flow from crystal clear springs at a rate of
seven to nine million gallons of water per day.
Alligators and turtles, as well as other creatures
make their home along the springs. Fishing
and boating help while away the lazy summer
Southern afternoons on the 28-acre lake.

Magnolia Springs is just one of many beautiful
Georgia state parks. Hamburg State Park is a
little more than a stone's throw away (about 60
miles) to the northwest and features a museum
with old agricultural displays. The restored 1921
water-powered grist mill turns out bags of corn
for visitors to purchase so they can make their
own genuine Southern cornbread.

Georgia Peach & Summer Fruit Salad

Makes 6 servings

Ingredients

¼ C. loosely packed fresh mint leaves

3 T. sugar

1¼ lbs. blackberries

3 ripe peaches, peeled, pitted and
cut into ½˝ slices

½ lb. seedless green grapes

Instructions

In a food processor, pulse mint and sugar until finely ground. In a large bowl combine fruit and sprinkle mint sugar over top; toss gently to combine. Chill or serve at room temperature.

Theme & Setting

The smells of sweet potato salad and southern fried chicken draw hungry friends and family to meet under the old magnolia tree for a picnic. Magnolia trees offer cool shade from the hot summer sun and the sweet aroma of mainly pink or white blossoms in the spring. Grown throughout the South and named after Pierre Magnol, a French botanist, the beloved magnolia represents nobility and dignity and has also been associated with beauty and perseverance.

Whether a warm summer day is beckoning you to step out into the sunshine, or a gloomy winter day makes you wish for a different season, this picnic menu will treat you to the tastes of a Southern kitchen. Dress the table with a calico or checked tablecloth. If outdoors, the scenery will be your centerpiece, and if indoors, use a canning jar as a vase to display garden flowers. Bluegrass or old-time gospel music will add to the ambiance as you Meet Under the Old Magnolia.

Corn Muffins with Honey Butter

Makes 2 dozen

Ingredients for muffins

2 C. flour

2 C. cornmeal

1 C. instant nonfat dry milk powder

¼ C. sugar

2 T. baking powder

1 tsp. salt

½ tsp. baking soda

2⅔ C. water

½ C. butter or margarine, melted

2 large eggs, beaten

1 T. lemon juice

Ingredients for honey butter

½ C. butter, softened

2 T. honey

Instructions

Preheat oven to 425°F. In a large bowl, combine flour, cornmeal, milk powder, sugar, baking powder, salt and baking soda. Add water, butter, eggs and lemon juice; stir until just combined. Fill greased or paper-lined muffin cups two-thirds full. Bake for 13 to 15 minutes or until golden. Cool for 5 minutes before removing from pan. In a small mixing bowl, beat together butter and honey. Serve muffins with honey butter on the side.

Oven-Fried Picnic Chicken

Makes 4 servings

Ingredients

¾ C. buttermilk or whole milk

1 tsp. lemon zest

¼ C. lemon juice

2 T. finely minced sweet onion

1 tsp. dried thyme

3 tsp. salt, divided

3 tsp. chili powder, divided

3½ to 4½ lbs. skinless chicken pieces*

⅔ C. grated Parmesan cheese

½ C. fine dry bread crumbs

½ C. cornmeal

3 T. minced fresh parsley

½ tsp. ground black pepper

2 large eggs

5 T. butter, melted, divided

Instructions

In a large bowl, whisk together milk, lemon zest, lemon juice, onion, thyme, 2 teaspoons salt and

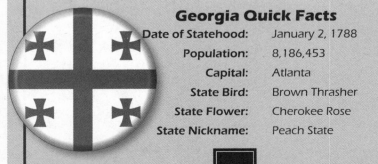

Georgia Quick Facts

Date of Statehood:	January 2, 1788
Population:	8,186,453
Capital:	Atlanta
State Bird:	Brown Thrasher
State Flower:	Cherokee Rose
State Nickname:	Peach State

2 teaspoons chili powder. Add chicken pieces and turn to coat. Cover the bowl of chicken and refrigerate for 2 to 4 hours. Preheat oven to 425°F. In a large shallow bowl, combine Parmesan cheese, bread crumbs, cornmeal, parsley, pepper, remaining 1 teaspoon salt and remaining 1 teaspoon chili powder; set aside. In a separate shallow bowl, whisk together eggs and 2 tablespoons melted butter. Remove chicken from marinade and lightly shake off excess. Dip chicken in egg mixture, then in cornmeal mixture to coat. Place chicken on a well-greased baking sheet, and drizzle with remaining 3 tablespoons butter. Bake for 35 to 40 minutes or until crisp, golden brown and cooked through. Chill to serve cold.

Chicken served cold retains better quality, and it is healthier, if prepared without the skin. If preferred, this dish can be prepared with skin on and/or served hot.

Sweet Potato Salad

Cherries and sweet potatoes are Georgia classics. In the South, sweet potatoes are often referred to as yams; although they share similarities, they are distinct. The fact that canned sweet potatoes are sometimes labeled as yams adds to the confusion of these two tubers. Either way you call it, this Southern salad made with sweet potatoes is sure to please.

Makes 4 to 6 servings

Ingredients for dressing
2 T. olive oil
1 T. pure maple syrup
1 T. orange juice
1 T. red wine or balsamic vinegar
½ T. lemon juice
1 tsp. peeled, minced fresh ginger
¼ tsp. ground cinnamon
⅛ tsp. ground nutmeg
Salt and pepper to taste

Ingredients for salad
2 lbs. red-skinned sweet potatoes, peeled, cut into ¾″ cubes
½ C. chopped green onions
½ C. chopped fresh parsley
½ C. toasted pecans*, coarsely chopped
½ C. dried cherries

Instructions
Steam sweet potatoes for 10 minutes or until just tender. Transfer sweet potatoes to a large bowl and cool to room temperature. In a small bowl, whisk dressing ingredients until well blended. In a large bowl, combine cooled sweet potatoes, green onions, parsley, pecans and dried cherries. Pour dressing over mixture and toss gently to coat. Salad can be made up to 2 hours ahead and served at room temperature.

To toast, place pecans in a single layer on a baking sheet. Bake at 350°F for approximately 10 minutes or until pecans are golden brown.

Pecan Pie Squares

Makes 36 pieces

Ingredients

⅔ C. sugar

½ C. butter or margarine, softened

2 tsp. vanilla extract, divided

1½ C. flour

⅔ C. brown sugar

½ C. light corn syrup

¼ tsp. salt

3 large eggs

1 C. coarsely chopped pecans

Instructions

Preheat oven to 350°F. Lightly grease bottom and sides of a 9 x 13″ baking pan. In a large bowl, mix sugar, butter and 1 teaspoon vanilla; stir in flour. Press dough in the bottom of a prepared baking pan, and ½″ up the sides. Bake for 15 to 17 minutes or until edges are light brown. Meanwhile, in a medium bowl, beat together brown sugar, corn syrup, remaining 1 teaspoon vanilla, salt and eggs with a spoon. Stir in pecans. Pour mixture over baked crust. Bake for an additional 25 to 30 minutes or until set. While still warm, loosen edges from sides of pan with a knife. Cool completely, about 1 hour. Cut into squares and serve.

Watermelon Lemonade

Makes 12 cups

Ingredients

8 C. cubed seedless or seeded watermelon

2 (12 oz.) cans frozen lemonade concentrate

4 C. water

Instructions

In a blender or food processor, blend watermelon until smooth. With a fine mesh strainer or cheesecloth, strain blended watermelon juice into a large pitcher. Add lemonade concentrate and water; stir to combine. Serve well chilled.

Food for Thought

- Pecans are native to the U.S. and were a staple of the Native American diet, especially throughout the winter. Commercial production of pecans was established in Georgia in the late 1800s. By the turn of the century, Georgia fell behind Mississippi and Louisiana in total acres of pecan trees, but today, Georgia is the top producer of the classic American food, pecans.

- Peaches were first grown in China almost 4,000 years ago, and they were first introduced along the Georgia coast in 1571 by Franciscan monks. Although Georgia falls behind South Carolina and California in peach production today, it's nicknamed the Peach State; Georgians would argue that their peaches are the sweetest and tastiest grown anywhere.

- Notable African contributions to Southern cuisine include okra and black-eyed peas, along with the popularity of deep-fried foods. The African method of cooking spinach greens was adapted to American turnip greens, kale, collards and mustard greens.

While in the Area

- Step on the stockade grounds of Camp Lawton, one of the largest Civil War prisons. Today, little remains except the history of what happened there. Magnolia Springs State Park shares this location where the earthen breastworks (prison fortifications) that once surrounded the prison can still be seen.

- Experience backcountry Georgia with a visit to Cumberland Island off the South Georgia coast. When you hike the trail under a canopy of oaks, you will see natural forest floors packed with palmetto, tidal creeks, freshwater wetlands, and man-made treasures like Plum Orchard Mansion and the First African Baptist Church. Hundreds of wild horses make the island their home, along with wild turkeys, armadillos and other creatures.

- Walk through the nation's largest registered Urban Historic Landmark District when you tour Savannah, the first planned city in America. Founded in 1733 by British General James Oglethorpe and known for its Southern charm and elegant architecture, Savannah is home to over 1,600 significant structures and retains 21 of the original 24 blocks of the city.

Ybor City, Tampa, Florida
Taste of Tapas – Culinary Art Entertainment

Party for Eight
Cuban Chicken Spread
Garlic & Pepper Shrimp
Diminuto Albondigas (Tiny Meatballs)
Piquillo Pepper Toasts
Cuban Sandwiches
Key Lime Tartlets
Soft Sangria Punch

About your Destination

Ybor City (pronounced like "EE-bohr") is the heart of Tampa's Latin Quarter and one of only two National Historic Landmark Districts in Florida. Founded in the 1880s by cigar manufacturers, the city became a thriving multi-ethnic home to thousands of Spanish, Cuban and Italian immigrants. The area experienced neglect through the decades following WWII, but has been beautifully redeveloped and restored to feature the red brick buildings, wrought iron balconies and narrow brick streets of its glory days. The nightlife, cuisine, shopping and historic richness of the area make it an inviting spot off the beaten path.

The greater Tampa area offers a broad sampling of Sunshine State fun; water, sand and surf are just the beginning. Busch Gardens, the Tampa Bay Performing Arts Center, major sporting

continued

Cuban Chicken Spread

Makes approximately 3 cups

Ingredients

1 C. chicken, boiled and ground
1 (4 oz.) jar red pimentos, drained
1 T. sweet pickle relish
½ (8 oz.) pkg. cream cheese, softened
2 hard-boiled eggs, chopped
½ C. mayonnaise
Assorted crackers or cocktail breads

Instructions

In a medium bowl, stir together first six ingredients until well combined. Serve with assorted crackers or cocktail breads.

Garlic & Pepper Shrimp

Makes 8 appetizer servings

Ingredients

1 C. olive oil
4 cloves garlic, minced
6 whole, dried red chiles
¼ C. minced flat-leaf fresh parsley
2 lbs. medium shrimp, shelled, deveined
Salt to taste
Crusty bread, optional

Instructions

In an extra large, deep skillet, heat olive oil over medium-high heat. Add garlic, chiles and parsley and cook, while stirring, for 10 seconds. Add shrimp and cook, for 3 to 4 minutes until pink and curled, stirring once. Season with salt and if desired, serve with crusty bread.

continued from page 62
events, Lowry Park Zoo (named #1 Zoo in the U.S. for kids), the Gasparilla Pirate Festival and dinner cruises on the Bay are just a few of the offerings.

Theme & Setting

Spanish influence in all of Florida was strong, as Spain laid the first claim on the region. The area of Ybor City had particularly strong ties to the culture. While additional ethnic cuisines can be enjoyed in Ybor City, especially Cuban foods, the popular Spanish Tapas of the city provides an especially fun way to entertain. Tapas originated in the motherland of Spain, as appetizers or small dishes to be enjoyed with drinks. Sometimes very simple tapas of olives, cheese cubes or meat bites are served; other times, more elaborate dishes like cold omelets, stuffed peppers or miniature sandwiches are featured.

Savoring the tastes of tapas throughout an entire evening is perhaps the finest way to enjoy them. Guests will enjoy culinary arts entertainment by watching the chef or participating in the cooking process. Organize the kitchen in advance by pre-measuring ingredients and making helpful lists. Serve tapas on casual, bright colored dishware and serve drinks in chunky, rustic glassware. Use a fruit bowl filled with colorful citrus and bright streamers of ribbon as your centerpiece. Add candlelight and set the tone with Spanish or Cuban music.

Diminuto Albondigas (Tiny Meatballs)

Makes approximately 80 pieces

Ingredients for meatballs

1 large onion, finely chopped
1 green bell pepper, minced
Olive oil for cooking
2 lbs. lean ground beef
½ lb. lean ground pork
⅔ C. fine dry bread crumbs
2½ tsp. salt
¼ tsp. ground nutmeg
¼ C. minced fresh parsley

Ingredients for sauce

4 large cloves garlic, minced
1 T. olive oil
1 (28 oz.) can whole tomatoes
¾ tsp. dried oregano, crumbled
Salt and pepper to taste

Instructions

To make meatballs: In a medium skillet over medium heat, sauté onion and bell pepper in small amount of oil until softened; allow to cool. In a large bowl, work together cooled onion mixture with remaining meatball ingredients. Form into tiny meatballs (approx. 1˝). In batches, heat a small amount of oil in a large skillet and work meatballs around to maintain shape and brown evenly. **To make sauce:** In a large heavy pot over medium-low heat, sauté garlic in oil until fragrant. Add tomatoes with juice and oregano; simmer, break up tomatoes and season with salt and pepper. **To make dish:** Add meatballs to sauce, cover, simmer and stir occasionally for 25 minutes or until meatballs are cooked through. Serve hot.

Piquillo Pepper Toasts

Makes 8 pieces

Ingredients

8 (½˝ thick) slices crusty Italian bread, crusts removed
Olive oil
1 large clove garlic, halved
¼ C. mild goat cheese, softened
Salt and pepper to taste
4 oz. (about ½ C.) Manchego or Parmesan cheese, grated
8 medium piquillo* peppers

Instructions

Preheat oven to 375°F. Arrange bread slices on a large baking sheet; brush with olive oil and bake for 8 minutes or until golden brown. Rub hot toasts with garlic. In a small bowl, season goat cheese with salt and pepper; mix until creamy. Spread a thin layer of cheese mixture on each toast; set aside. In a shallow bowl, dredge peppers in grated cheese. In a large nonstick skillet over medium heat, cook coated peppers for about 2 minutes per side or until browned and crisp. Transfer peppers to toasts and serve.

*Piquillos are slow roasted sweet, smoky and slightly spicy Spanish peppers, available in specialty markets by the jar or can. Roasted red bell peppers can substitute for piquillos.

Cuban Sandwiches

"Cubano" stands, called loncherias, *serve Cuban sandwiches along the streets of Tampa. Authentic sandwiches are served on Cuban bread, similar to a French loaf, but made with sweeter, egg-based dough; they include roast pork, ham, cheese and pickle. Serve whole sandwiches as a meal or make slices part of a tapas menu.* **The recipe for Cuban Roast Pork will yield more than is needed, so enjoy it as a tasty leftover.**

<u>*Makes 1 Sandwich (8 appetizer slices)*</u>

Ingredients for Cuban roast pork

3 to 4 lbs. pork shoulder roast, trimmed

3 cloves garlic, slivered

½ C. orange juice

½ C. lime juice

1 T. ground oregano

1 tsp. ground cumin

1 tsp. ground black pepper, or to taste

1 T. salt, or to taste

1 large onion, sliced

Ingredients for sandwiches

1 (8˝) loaf Cuban bread (or other crusty, soft-centered loaf)

Butter for spreading

Dill pickle slices

¼ lb. prepared Cuban roast pork, pieced or sliced

¼ lb. baked ham, sliced

⅛ lb. mild Swiss cheese

Yellow mustard, optional

Instructions

To make roast pork: Cut slits in surface of meat and insert slivers of garlic. In a large sealable plastic bag, combine remaining ingredients; seal and shake gently until well mixed. Add roast to the bag, seal and refrigerate overnight. Preheat oven to 275°F. Remove roast and place in a large covered baking dish; discard bag and marinade. Roast for 4 to 5 hours, turning once while baking. Allow to cool slightly before slicing or pulling into pieces to serve or use in Cuban Sandwiches. **To make sandwiches:** Slice loaf of bread lengthwise; spread butter on the insides of both pieces. Assemble sandwich in the following order: bottom bread slice, pickles, roast pork, ham, cheese and if desired, spread mustard on top piece of bread before setting on sandwich. Preheat lightly greased sandwich press*, pancake griddle or extra large skillet; add sandwich and press down to flatten to half its original thickness. (If using a griddle or skillet, smash with a heated heavy cast-iron skillet.) Grill for 2 to 3 minutes per side, until cheese is melted and bread is golden. Slice to serve.

*Cuban sandwiches are pressed while cooking on a flat surface. Special sandwich presses are available, but be aware that the common panini sandwich press creates grill marks that would not be present on a true Cuban sandwich.

Key Lime Tartlets

Although these sweet bites are not Spanish in origin, they fit into a Florida tapas party well, as they feature the wonderful Florida Key lime. The recipe yields extra Key lime filling (also defined as curd); serve leftovers with biscuits or bread.

<u>Makes 30 to 36 tartlets</u>

Ingredients

4 large eggs
⅔ C. fresh Key lime juice
⅔ C. sugar
6 T. unsalted butter, melted
2 tsp. grated Key lime zest
30 to 36 (2″) tartlet shells
    or 8 to 12 (4″) tart shells*
Whipped cream, optional
Sliced strawberries, optional

Instructions

In a medium saucepan over medium-low heat, whisk together eggs, Key lime juice, sugar, and butter. While continuously whisking, cook for 12 minutes or until mixture has thickened. Stir in lime zest. Gently pour mixture through a fine mesh strainer, discard solids and refrigerate

covered lime filling for 4 to 6 hours. Spoon filling into tart shells and top with whipped cream or strawberries, if desired.

Purchase pre-made tart shells in the frozen or bakery sections of the supermarket, or to bake from scratch: Pulse together 1¼ C. flour, ¾ C. cake flour, 1½ T. sugar, ¾ tsp. salt and ¼ tsp. baking powder. Add 1 C. softened butter and ¼ C. shortening; pulse until crumbly. Add 6 T. cold water, 1 T. at a time. Remove dough and wrap in plastic; chill a minimum of 2 hours. Shape into balls and press lightly into tart pan; prick with fork and bake at 375°F for 13 minutes or until golden. Remove from pans and cool on wire racks.

Florida Quick Facts

Date of Statehood:	March 3, 1845
Population:	15,982,378
Capital:	Tallahassee
State Bird:	Mockingbird
State Flower:	Orange blossom
State Nickname:	Sunshine State

Soft Sangria Punch

Sangria wine is paired with Spanish tapas, but this non–alcoholic punch is a refreshing alternative.

<u>Makes 10 to 12 servings</u>

Ingredients

1⅓ C. lemon juice, strained
⅔ C. orange juice, strained
½ C. sugar
64 oz. grape or cranberry juice, or combination
Sliced lemons, oranges or other fresh fruit
Ice, optional

Instructions

Chill juices. In a large container, combine lemon juice, orange juice and sugar; stir until sugar dissolves. Add grape or cranberry juice; garnish with fresh fruits. Serve from a glass pitcher or punch bowl. If desired, add ice.

Food for Thought

• One reason Florida has a diverse cuisine is the geographical stretch of the state from Georgia to just 90 miles from Cuba. Both Creole and Cajun cooking influence the North, while the South is swayed by the Caribbean cultures. Cuban, Jamaican, Dominican, Bahamian, Oriental, Haitian, Columbian, Puerto Rican and many more cultures play a hand in the diverse Floridian palate.

• *Sopas,* or soups, are popular in Spain and Cuba. Black bean soup, prepared with ham hocks and sometimes served over rice, is a Cuban specialty. A pureed mixture of tomatoes and other raw vegetables combine to create cold Gazpacho (soup), which originated in Spain.

• Florida is the largest orange and citrus fruit-producing state in the U.S; therefore citrus flavors are found in many dishes there. Key limes thrive in the Florida Keys region, giving them their name. They are smaller, rounder, more yellow and sweeter than the familiar Persian lime.

While in the Area

• Watch demonstrations of cigars being hand-rolled at the Ybor City State Museum. The cigar industry was at the heart of the original city, which was named after Vicente Martinez Ybor, a prominent Spanish-born cigar manufacturer. The museum offers many other displays of historical significance as well.

• Hear an eclectic blend of music in one of the many nightclubs of Ybor City. The Latin, jazz, blues, salsa, reggae and hip-hop music played for the crowds livens the atmosphere.

• Catch a ride to one of the fabulous restaurants of the area in a pedi-cab, a bicycle built for three but pedaled by one.

New Orleans, Louisiana
Balconies & Porches, Streetcars & Carriages

*Luncheon and Afternoon Coffee
for Four to Eight*
Salad of the South *with*
Creole Honey Mustard Vinaigrette
Fried Green Tomatoes & Shrimp Remoulade
Jambalaya of the Delta
Beignets (Donuts)
Southern Girl Pralines
Chicory Café au Lait

About your Destination

Louisiana's interesting history began long before the 1803 Louisiana Purchase (a great bargain costing $15 million for more than a million square miles); it continues through the more recent challenge of Hurricane Katrina and her resulting devastation. The state offers hunting, fishing, canoeing and waterskiing as a few of the many outdoor recreational opportunities. It is also home to big sports teams like the basketball-wielding Hornets and the football-playing Saints. The sounds of Louisiana are unique, with the invention of jazz in New Orleans and the rural bayou origins of zydeco. But, what Louisiana seems to be best known for is its food. Cajun and

continued

Salad of the South with Creole Honey Mustard Vinaigrette

Makes 8 servings

Ingredients

1 T. vegetable oil
1 C. dry roasted peanuts
Salt and pepper to taste
Cayenne pepper to taste
¼ C. Creole (or other spicy) mustard
2 T. honey
¼ C. apple cider vinegar
1 C. olive oil
20 to 24 oz. assorted mixed greens

Instructions

In a large skillet, heat vegetable oil over medium-high heat. Fry peanuts for about 1 minute, until golden. Drain peanuts and season with salt and cayenne pepper; set aside. In a large bowl, whisk together mustard, honey and vinegar. Add salt and pepper to taste and then slowly add oil while whisking. Continue to whisk until well combined. Toss greens with dressing to taste. Divide on individual serving plates and sprinkle with peanuts to serve.

continued from page 68
Creole cooking... uniquely and excitedly delicious!

Theme & Setting

The open balconies overlooking the French Quarter and the grand porches of stately Southern homes of the Garden District, represent the magnificent architecture of the city of New Orleans. Streetcars and carriages continue to provide transportation with Southern charm for visitors today. New Orleans is the center of Creole cooking. Although the restaurants, cafes, markets, bakeries and bistros of New Orleans are remarkable, great Southern cooking is found in the home. Invite friends to a Louisiana meal served up in the "Southern" comfort of your home, at a formal dining table or on the porch or veranda. Guests will feel as though they stepped off the streetcar on St. Charles Avenue when you welcome them to your lace-topped table adorned with a vase holding peonies or spring blooms. Serve your luncheon on elegant china and follow the meal with famous French Beignets and Café au Lait. From the receipt of a hand-written invitation to their departure with a party favor of wrapped pralines, your guests' will enjoy their time spent in the South.

Fried Green Tomatoes & Shrimp Remoulade

Remoulade is an example of the French influence in New Orleans.

<u>*Makes 8 appetizer servings*</u>

Ingredients for remoulade

½ C. Creole (or other spicy) mustard

2 T. ketchup

1 tsp. Worcestershire sauce

2 tsp. prepared horseradish

1 tsp. minced garlic

1 tsp. fresh lemon juice

1½ tsp. paprika

¼ tsp. ground white pepper

⅛ tsp. ground black pepper

⅛ tsp. cayenne pepper

Salt to taste

½ C. olive oil

¼ C. finely chopped celery hearts

1½ tsp. finely chopped fresh parsley

1 T. grated onion

1 T. finely chopped green onion, white part only

Hot sauce, optional

Ingredients for dish

1 C. buttermilk

1 egg

4 to 6 T. vegetable oil

8 slices green tomato, about ½″ thick

1 C. corn flour*

Salt and pepper to taste

24 medium shrimp, poached, peeled and chilled

Spinach leaves for plate liner

Instructions

To make remoulade: In a large bowl, combine the first 10 ingredients and salt to taste; mix well. Add olive oil in a slow stream while whisking. Add remaining remoulade ingredients and mix well. If desired, stir in hot sauce. Cover and chill before serving.

To make tomatoes: In a medium bowl, whisk together buttermilk and egg. In a large skillet, heat oil over medium heat. Place corn flour in a shallow dish and season with salt and pepper to taste. Dip tomato slices in egg mixture, then coat with corn flour. Cook slices in oil, for 1½ to 2 minutes per side or until golden brown and cooked through, but not mushy.

To assemble dish: Line individual serving plates with spinach leaf liner. Add a warm tomato slice and top with 3 chilled shrimp. Spoon 1½ tablespoons chilled remoulade sauce over the shrimp.

Note: *Sauce can be stored covered and refrigerated for up to 1 week.*

*Corn flour is finely ground cornmeal. Coarser cornmeal or all-purpose flour can be used in place of corn flour.

Jambalaya of the Delta

Makes 8 servings

Ingredients

4 T. olive oil, divided

1 lb. medium shrimp, peeled and deveined

Creole seasoning* to taste

1½ lbs. boneless, skinless chicken breasts

1½ lbs. andouille sausage, cut into ½″ cubes

2 C. chopped onion

1 C. chopped celery

1 C. chopped red or green bell pepper

2 T. minced garlic

3 bay leaves

¼ tsp. cayenne pepper

1½ T. chopped thyme leaves

1 C. chopped tomatoes

6 C. water

2 C. uncooked rice

Salt and pepper to taste

1 C. chopped green onions

½ C. chopped fresh parsley

Instructions

In a large Dutch oven, heat 2 tablespoons of olive oil over medium heat. Season shrimp with Creole seasoning to taste. Sauté shrimp for about 4 minutes or until almost cooked through. Using a slotted spoon, remove shrimp; set aside. Season chicken breasts with Creole seasoning to taste. Add remaining 2 tablespoons oil to Dutch oven; when hot, add chicken. Cook for about 4 minutes per side or until lightly browned and just cooked through; remove and set aside. Add sausage to Dutch oven and cook until browned. Add onion, celery, bell pepper, garlic, bay leaves, cayenne pepper and thyme; cook for about 6 minutes or until vegetables are softened. Meanwhile, cut cooked chicken into ½″ to 1″ pieces. Add chicken, tomatoes and water to sausage-vegetable mixture; season with salt and pepper, cover and simmer for 20 minutes. Add rice, stir well and return to a boil. Reduce heat to low, cover and cook for 15 minutes. Stir in shrimp, green onions and parsley; cover and cook for an additional 10 minutes. Allow to stand for 10 minutes before serving.

To make your own Creole seasoning, combine 2½ T. paprika, 2 T. garlic powder, 2 T. salt and 1 T. each of black pepper, onion powder, cayenne pepper, dried oregano and dried thyme.

Louisiana Quick Facts

Date of Statehood:	April 30, 1812
Population:	4,468,976
Capital:	Baton Rouge
State Bird:	Eastern Brown Pelican
State Flower:	Magnolia
State Nickname:	Pelican State

Beignets (Donuts)

A beignet, pronounced bĕn-yā´, is a specialty of New Orleans. The pastry, which is deep-fried and served hot, gets its name from the French word for fritter. Sweet beignets dusted with powdered sugar seem to be the traditional favorite, but savory beignets made with herbs or crabmeat are also popular.

Makes approximately 30 small donuts

Ingredients

1¼ tsp. active dry yeast
¼ C. sugar
¾ C. warm water (110°F)
½ tsp. salt
1 large egg, well beaten
½ C. evaporated milk
3½ C. flour, divided
2 T. vegetable shortening
Canola oil for deep-frying
Powdered sugar

Instructions

In a large bowl, mix yeast, sugar and warm water; stir and let stand for 10 minutes until very foamy. Beat in salt, egg and milk; beat in half the flour, and then add shortening, and beat until smooth. Add remaining flour, ½ cup at a time, mixing well after each addition. Turn dough out onto floured surface and knead, about a dozen turns, until smooth. Add more flour if necessary to prevent sticking. Place dough in oiled bowl, cover and refrigerate for 2 to 12 hours. Divide dough into three pieces. Roll out each piece, on a lightly floured surface, to 15˝ to 20˝ rectangle, ¼˝ to ½˝ thick. Cut into 10 rectangles, about 1½˝ x 2˝. In a deep fryer, electric skillet or deep skillet, heat 2 to 3˝ oil to 350°F. Fry four at a time for 1 to 2 minutes per side until lightly browned and puffed up. Drain on paper towel-lined plate. Dust with powdered sugar to serve.

Southern Girl Pralines

Makes approximately 2 pounds

Ingredients

1⅓ C. sugar
⅔ C. brown sugar
1⅓ C. water or sherry
⅛ tsp. salt
2 to 3 C. pecans halves

Instructions

In a large heavy pan over medium low heat, combine first four ingredients and bring to a boil. Cover and cook for about 3 minutes; uncover and cook to the soft-ball stage of 234°F. Remove pan from heat and cool candy to 110°F. Beat mixture until it thickens and begins to lose its gloss. Stir in pecans. By the heaping tablespoon, drop candies onto a buttered platter. When hardened, wrap individually in foil. Store in an airtight container.

Food for Thought

- Many people believe Creole and Cajun to be the same; however, they are different in origin and taste. Cajun cuisine was derived from the rustic or provincial French cooking of the Acadian (Cajun) people in the more rural areas of Louisiana. Creole cuisine developed in the city and on larger plantations. Creole dishes tend to be more cream- and butter-based, while Cajun cooking features a dark roux and includes dishes like dirty rice, fried catfish or crawfish étouffée.

- In rural areas of Louisiana, you can order up some smothered or fried frog legs.

- Oyster bars are a New Orleans tradition. Some say oysters served on the half shell are as "naturally New Orleans" as Red Beans and Rice or Café au Lait and Beignets.

- Red Beans and Rice is a favorite in the South, especially Louisiana. One famous New Orleans jazz musician, Louis Armstrong, even signed his letters, "Red beans and ricely yours."

While in the Area

- Explore the Mississippi River on the Paddlewheeler Creole Queen. She took her maiden voyage in 1983, and although she would be at home in the New Orleans of the 1800s, the safety, luxury and comfort of the modern boat, is definitely enjoyed by today's guests.

- Listen to Dixieland Jazz, the original jazz music of New Orleans. Blues, ragtime and other influences like brass band traditions, came together in this unique style of music.

- Dance to the tunes of Zydeco music. This Cajun style of music and dance developed in the rural bayou areas of Louisiana; the Acadians blended fiddle, accordion and bass sounds into a lively folk music, unique unto itself.

- Celebrate Mardi Gras on famous Bourbon Street. Music, parades, picnics, floats and excitement are all part of the big holiday tradition on Fat Tuesday.

Chicory Café au Lait

Chicory is an endive relative with curly, bitter-tasting leaves, often eaten as salad or cooked greens. In the South, chicory roots are roasted and ground to be used as a coffee substitute. Chicory coffee can be found in most supermarkets and is stronger than regular coffee. If a chicory blend is unavailable to you, brew extra strong coffee to serve as *café au lait*, French for "coffee with milk." Warm heavy whipping cream, half and half or whole milk in a small saucepan and add it to the hot chicory coffee. Offer sugar cubes with the café au lait.

Fort Davis, Texas
The Lone Star, Beneath a Multitude of Stars

Supper for Eight
Texas Caviar with Baked Tortilla Chips
Jalapeño Cornbread
Easy Texas Chili
Blackberry Cobbler
Southern Sweet Tea

About your Destination

The Lone Star State nickname comes from the single golden star that appeared on the blue background of the first Texas flag. It originally symbolized independence from Mexico and the struggle required to obtain it. Several versions of the Texas flag have been flown over the years, always displaying a lone star. The current flag contains a red and white stripe on the right and a single white five-point star over blue on the left.

One Texan soldier of the Mexican War, Belgian immigrant Deidrick Dutchover, played an important role in the history of Fort Davis, near the small settlement of Chihuahua (which later became the town of Fort Davis). Dutchover was assigned to guard Fort Davis when the Civil War broke out. After Apaches invaded, he made an 80-mile, four-day journey by foot, while protecting a small group of people including a woman and children. Dutchover later returned

continued

Texas Caviar

Makes 8 to 12 servings

Ingredients

½ onion, chopped

1 bunch green onions, chopped

1 green bell pepper, chopped

2 jalapeño peppers, chopped

1 T. minced garlic

1 pt. cherry tomatoes, quartered

1 (15 oz.) can black beans, drained

1 (15 oz.) can black-eyed peas, drained

½ tsp. ground coriander

1 C. Italian dressing

1 bunch fresh cilantro, chopped

Instructions

In a large bowl, combine both onions, both peppers, garlic, tomatoes, black beans and, black-eyed peas. In a medium bowl, whisk together coriander and dressing. Stir dressing into vegetable mixture until evenly combined. Cover and refrigerate for a minimum of 2 hours to allow flavors to blend. Stir and toss with desired amount of cilantro. Serve with tortilla chips.

continued from page 74

to Fort Davis, and the town began to boom in 1867 due to its location at the crossroads of two important trails. Fort Davis is a popular destination for tourists today, where three major attractions include: Fort Davis, now a National Historic Site; the arboretum, opened by the Chihuahuan Desert Research Institute; and the University of Texas McDonald Observatory, in the nearby Davis Mountains.

Theme & Setting

The Lone Star State of Texas lies beneath a multitude of stars in the heavens. The McDonald Observatory, equipped with four amazing research telescopes, makes star gazing a pleasure. Its location atop Mount Locke provides prime viewing opportunities, as the night skies of the West Texas Davis Mountains are some of the darkest in the continental U.S.

Plan a night-sky viewing of your own as you gather around a Texan feast. Decorate with stars, moons or other symbols of the universe, and display of the Lone Star State flag. After eating chili and cornbread, gaze up at the heavens to identify constellations. Check out simple astronomy books from the local library and drive away from city lights to observe darker skies. Or, plan a party to coincide with your local observatory's hours or special events. Even if you don't make it outside to view the sky, you will be the star for cooking up a Lone Star feast.

Baked Tortilla Chips

Makes 8 to 12 servings

Ingredients
24 (6˝) white corn tortillas, divided
2 T. vegetable oil, divided
Fine-grain salt

Instructions
Preheat oven to 350°F. Working in two batches, brush both sides of half the tortillas with 1 tablespoon oil. Stack tortillas and cut into sixths to make chips. Spread pieces out in a single layer on 2 large baking sheets and sprinkle with salt. Bake for 12 to 15 minutes or until golden brown and crisp, rotating baking sheets once. Repeat with remaining tortillas and salt. Serve with Texas Caviar, dip or salsa.

Jalapeño Cornbread

Makes 9 pieces

Ingredients
1½ C. cornmeal
½ C. flour
6 T. sugar
2 tsp. baking powder
1 tsp. salt
½ tsp. baking soda
2 large eggs
1 C. buttermilk
¼ C. olive oil
3 jalapeño peppers, seeded and finely chopped

Instructions
Preheat oven to 400°F. In a large bowl, combine cornmeal, flour, sugar, baking powder, salt and baking soda. In a separate large bowl, whisk together eggs, buttermilk and oil. Add dry ingredients to egg mixture and stir just until moistened. Fold in peppers. Pour into a greased 9˝ square baking pan. Bake for 20 to 22 minutes or until a wooden toothpick inserted in the center comes out clean. Cut into squares or wedges and serve warm.

TEXAS QUICK FACTS

Date of Statehood:	December 29, 1845
Population:	20,851,820
Capital:	Austin
State Bird:	Mockingbird
State Flower:	Bluebonnet
State Nickname:	Lone Star State

Easy Texas Chili

Chunks of steak rather than ground meat, as well as the lack of beans, make this chili recipe Texan. This "easy" version uses purchased chili powder for convenience, but for an even more authentic Texan taste, homemade chili powder can substitute. Many chili lovers will claim that the dish originated in their own state, but plenty of Texans would argue that unequivocally, the Lone Star State was the starting point.

Makes 8 servings

Ingredients

2 T. vegetable oil

3 lbs. boneless beef chuck, cut in 1″cubes

1 large onion, chopped

1½ tsp. minced garlic

2 tsp. cornmeal

3 T. chili powder

1 T. ground cumin

1 T. dried oregano

3 C. beef broth

1 C. tomato puree

1½ tsp. salt

½ tsp. ground black pepper

½ tsp. cayenne pepper

Jalapeño peppers, canned or fresh, optional

Water, as needed

Instructions

In a large pot over medium-high heat, sear beef in heated oil until browned; work in batches if necessary. Add onions to seared beef; sauté for 5 minutes. Add garlic and cornmeal; cook for 1 minute. Add chili powder, cumin, oregano, broth, tomato puree, salt, both peppers and, if desired, jalapeño peppers. Bring mixture to a boil. Reduce heat to low; simmer for 1½ hours, stirring occasionally. Add water during cooking, to thin if necessary. Serve hot.

Blackberry Cobbler

Makes 8 servings

Ingredients

1¼ C. sugar, divided

1 C. self-rising flour

1 C. milk

½ C. butter, melted

2½ C. blackberries, fresh or frozen, thawed

Extra sugar, optional

Vanilla ice cream, optional

Instructions

Preheat oven to 350°F and grease 9 x 13″ baking dish. In a large bowl, combine 1 cup sugar and flour. Whisk in milk and then butter, until well blended. Spread batter evenly in baking dish. Sprinkle with berries and remaining ¼ cup sugar. (Cobbler mixture will be shallow in the pan.) Bake for 45 to 55 minutes or until lightly golden and wooden toothpick inserted in center comes out clean. If desired, sprinkle 1 teaspoon sugar over cobbler 10 minutes before baking is finished. Spoon into dishes to serve warm. If desired, top with ice cream.

Southern Sweet Tea

Iced tea is a great Texan refresher, because temperatures can climb to 120° F during the hot summer months. It's a tradition in the South, where it is unthinkable to drink unsweetened tea.

Makes 1 gallon

Ingredients

6 C. plus additional water
4 family-size tea bags
1 to 1¾ C. sugar

Instructions

In a saucepan, bring 6 cups water to a boil; add tea bags. Boil for 1 minute; remove from heat. Cover and steep for 10 minutes. Remove tea bags, squeezing gently. Add sugar, stirring until dissolved. Pour into a 1-gallon pitcher and add enough water to fill. Serve over ice.

Food for Thought

- Texas cuisine can be categorized into three main groupings: Chili, Barbecue and Tex-Mex. Annual chili cook-offs highlight one-, two- and three-alarm chilis; they like it hot in Texas. Beef is the focus of BBQ in the state, as Texas produces more beef than any other state. And Tex-Mex is a wonderful hybrid menu influenced by the cultures of Texas and Mexico and their tasty blend of flavors.

- Beans are a staple of Texas, where pintos are most common. Beans are served boiled, baked, mashed, fried and re-fried. Ironically, most Texas chili is served without beans.

- Chicken fried steak is popular in Texas. A big piece of inexpensive steak is beaten until tender, dipped in batter, deep-fried and buried under a puddle of cream gravy. This is the comfort food of a true Texan.

While in the Area

- Drive a couple dozen miles out of Fort Davis to view one of the mysteries of the Texan skies: the Marfa lights. Featured on *Unsolved Mysteries* and studied by *National Geographic,* these anomalies of the sky have been written about for decades and talked about for even longer. Although described in different ways, descriptions usually include spherical-shaped lights that glow softly like stars, which intensify and fade. Movement is sometimes reported to be rapid and color is generally reddish and orange. An official viewing area has been provided nine miles east of Marfa, Texas, along Highway 90. The mysterious lights remain unexplained.

- Hike the trails or canyon next to Keesey Creek in Davis Mountains State Park. The scenic park offers 1,000 feet of change in elevation within its borders. Stop by the interpretive center for some information.

- Wind your way along the 75-mile Scenic Loop Drive. It starts at Fort Davis, passes McDonald Observatory, continues through the mountains with broad views of the Rio Grande, and takes you back to your starting point. It has been described as one of the most scenic but unrecognized drives in Texas and America.

Albuquerque, New Mexico
Pop's Route 66 Diner

Casual Dinner or Lunch for Eight
Burgers of the Southwest
Salsa Verde (Green Chile Sauce)
Ma's Coleslaw
Chile Con Queso Fries
Black Cows & Old Fashioned Sodas

Another Taste of New Mexico
New Mexican Breakfast Burrito

About your Destination

U.S. Highway 66, popularly known as "Route 66," was a ribbon of highway snaking its way through eight states to connect Chicago and Los Angeles. It was also the first all-weather highway to cross the western United States. The famed highway was officially commissioned in 1926 and completed more than a decade later, with an official count of 2,448 miles of road. The popularity of Route 66 grew in the 1950s with the growth of a new phenomenon, the family vacation, which also became a symbol of the optimism that grew during the post WWII era. But Route 66 became hard to find after bigger highways took its place and its markers came down with its decommissioning in 1985. Since that time, individuals, groups and finally the

continued

Burgers of the Southwest

Makes 8 servings

Ingredients

2 T. butter, divided

2 lbs. ground beef (90% or leaner)

Salt and pepper to taste

8 slices pepper jack cheese, optional

2 C. Green Chile Sauce, warmed

8 soft hamburger buns, split

Optional condiments, such as leaf lettuce, tomatoes, onions, pickles, ketchup, mustard and crispy bacon

Instructions

In a large heavy skillet over medium-high heat, heat 1 tablespoon butter until melted and hot, but not browning. Add the buns, cut-side down, and toast until golden. Set aside. Gently form ground beef into eight flat patties about ½″ thick. Season with salt and pepper. Work in two batches to cook patties, or use two skillets at the same time. Melt ½ tablespoon butter in the skillet per four-burger batch. Add burgers when butter is hot, but not browning. Cook patties, without moving them, for 3 minutes, until a thick crust forms on the underside. Turn burgers over and cook for another 3 to 5 minutes, or until done. If desired, flip over once more and add optional cheese, allowing it to melt for 30 to 60 seconds. Place patties on a serving platter, and serve with Green Chile Sauce, toasted buns and optional condiments.

continued from page 80

government itself have made efforts to preserve its history and value.

Albuquerque is just one of the great towns along the route. The ethnic diversity and Southwestern culture is remarkable, with Pueblo- and Spanish-inspired architecture, art fairs, music and dance festivals, and world-famous cuisine.

Theme & Setting

The "cats" (hip people) will "flip" (get very excited), when you invite them for dinner and music as you play the "sides" (vinyl records) and do the "twist." The 50s diner is an icon of the American past and Route 66, as checkerboard floors and barstool-lined soda counters were a familiar stop along the highway.

Recreate the diner as you serve up homemade "pops" in soda glasses, and play the music of the past. Invite your guests to dress in 50s attire, and serve your food in plastic paper-lined baskets. Other ideas include decorating with old records, using Route 66 symbol on your invitations and posting homemade road signs around the room. The menu has been planned to represent the classic diner experience, as well as the Southwest flair of the cuisine in Albuquerque. So, lace up your saddle shoes and come along for a "cloud nine" (really happy) time.

Salsa Verde (Green Chile Sauce)

Makes 3 cups

Ingredients

1 lb. tomatillos*, husks removed

1 lb. poblano peppers, halved with stems, seeds and membranes removed

2 T. vegetable oil

½ large onion, chopped

1 clove garlic, minced

2 T. flour

1½ C. chicken broth

¼ tsp. dried oregano

¼ tsp. ground cumin

1 tsp. salt

¼ tsp. ground black pepper

Instructions

In a large pot, bring salted water to a boil. Add tomatillos, cover and return to a boil. Boil for 5 minutes, then drain. Process tomatillos in a food processor or blender until smooth. Preheat broiler. Meanwhile, flatten peppers with the skin-side up, on an aluminum foil-lined baking sheet. Broil peppers until skin has bubbled and blackened. Remove from oven and fold edges of foil over to create a packet; seal and let rest for 5 minutes. Peel off and discard skins. Add peppers to tomatillos and process again until smooth. Meanwhile, in a large pot, heat oil on medium. Add onion and garlic; cook until soft and lightly golden. Stir in flour and cook while stirring for 1 minute. Slowly incorporate broth, one tablespoon at a time. Stir in the tomatillo-poblano mixture and remaining ingredients. Bring to a boil while stirring. Reduce heat to low and simmer for 30 minutes. Serve warm with hot dishes or cooled with chips.

Tomatillos are a Mexican relative of the tomato with the appearance of a little green tomato covered with a husk. They are often available in the supermarket or in Latin food markets.

New Mexico Quick Facts

Date of Statehood:	January 6, 1912
Population:	1,819,046
Capital:	Santa Fe
State Bird:	Roadrunner
State Flower:	Yucca Flower
State Nickname:	Land of Enchantment

Ma's Coleslaw

Makes 8 small servings

Ingredients

½ large head green cabbage

3 green onions, green portion removed

¼ C. minced green bell pepper

¼ C. minced red bell pepper

1 medium carrot, peeled and minced

½ C. cider vinegar

1 tsp. salt

2 tsp. sugar

½ C. low-fat or regular sour cream

½ C. low-fat or regular mayonnaise

Instructions

Cut cabbage into ⅛″ shreds and place in a large bowl. Finely chop green onions and stir into cabbage with peppers and carrots. In a separate medium bowl, whisk vinegar, salt, sugar, sour cream and mayonnaise until smooth. Pour dressing over vegetables and mix well. Serve immediately, or cover and refrigerate for later use.

Chile Con Queso Fries

Makes 8 servings

Ingredients

1 (26 oz.) bag frozen French fries

1 C. shredded American cheese

½ C. shredded sharp Cheddar cheese

¼ C. half & half, more if needed

1 medium tomato, chopped

1 green chile, chopped*

⅛ tsp. garlic powder

Instructions

Cook French fries according to package instructions. Meanwhile, in heavy medium saucepan, slowly melt cheeses over low heat. Add ¼ cup half & half while stirring constantly. Stir in tomato, chile and garlic powder. To reach desired consistency, add more cream if necessary. Spread fries on serving platter and serve con queso drizzled on top or as a dipping sauce on the side.

French fries from scratch: Three large russet potatoes make enough fries for 4 servings. Cut potatoes lengthwise in ¼″ "square" strips. Soak cut potatoes in water for 1 hour to remove starch. Heat vegetable oil to 325°F and partially cook them for 5 minutes until very soft but not brown. Remove from oil and drain on paper towels. Increase oil temperature to 375°F. Return potatoes to oil and cook until crisp and golden brown. Remove from oil and drain again; season with salt immediately.

Chile amount may be adjusted for personal preference.

Black Cows and Old Fashioned Sodas

Makes 1 serving

Ingredients for Black Cow

3 T. chocolate syrup
10 oz. root beer
1 to 2 scoops vanilla ice cream

Instructions for Black Cow

Pour chocolate syrup in the bottom of a tall glass. Pour root beer over chocolate until glass is half full. Add desired amount of ice cream. Add remainder of root beer and serve with a straw and spoon.

Ingredients and Instructions for Basic Soda

Combine 1 to 3 ounces flavored syrup* with 10 oz. club soda or seltzer water in a glass, stir, add ice (or ice cream), and serve with a straw (and spoon, if needed).

Suggested Soda Combinations

Cola + cherry syrup + vanilla syrup = Cherry Cream Coke

Cola + chocolate syrup + vanilla syrup = Chocolate Cream Coke

Cola + cherry syrup + chocolate syrup = Cherry Chocolate Coke

Lemon-lime soda + watermelon syrup = Fruity Soda

Flavored syrups can be purchased in specialty kitchen shops, through online vendors or sometimes from the supermarket where they may be displayed near the coffee.

New Mexican Breakfast Burrito

Makes 4 servings

Ingredients

6 T. oil, divided
1 red bell pepper, seeded, coarsely chopped
1 green bell pepper, seeded, coarsely chopped
½ medium onion, coarsely chopped
1½ lbs. chorizo (Mexican sausage), removed from casing
12 large eggs, beaten
4 (10″ or larger) flour tortillas
Red or green salsa, optional

Instructions

In a large skillet over medium-high heat, heat 2 tablespoons oil. Sauté peppers and onion until soft; transfer to a dish and set aside. In a large skillet over medium heat, cook chorizo in 4 tablespoons oil until cooked through. Add peppers and onions to chorizo and pour in beaten eggs. Stir to scramble while cooking over medium heat, until eggs are just set and still have a wet look to their exterior, or to preferred doneness. Set aside briefly while heating tortillas. Divide egg and chorizo mixture between the four tortillas and wrap as a burrito. If desired, drizzle with optional salsa.

Food for Thought

- New Mexican cuisine began as a unique blend of Native American classics such as blue corn and squash, with ingredients such as chile peppers, wheat flour and pork.

- The smoke-kissed flavor of freshly roasted green chiles and the earthy fruitiness of red chile sauce are essential in the cooking of New Mexican cuisine.

- Authentic Native American tastes can be shared at the Indian Pueblo Cultural Center in Albuquerque, where you can enjoy samples of fry bread, posole (hominy stew with chiles) and other traditional foods.

- Spanish missionaries introduced the first grapevines to the Rio Grande Valley in New Mexico, in 1629. Albuquerque restaurants serve award-winning local wines alongside the unique New Mexican cuisine.

While in the Area

- Board the Rail Runner Express to travel over the famed Atchison, Topeka and Santa Fe Railway tracks, distinctively known as the Santa Fe. The new express will take you from Albuquerque to Santa Fe to see the museums, galleries, shops and famous Santa Fe Plaza, where you can stop for a bite in a great Southwestern restaurant.

- Photograph a rising beauty at the annual hot air balloon festival in Albuquerque. You will see more than 700 balloons in the sky at what is considered to be the most photographed event in the world, drawing a huge international crowd of balloonists and spectators.

- Bicycle on awesome mountain trails or enjoy a wide range of outdoor activities such as skiing, golfing, hiking and mountaineering, which offer the enjoyment of New Mexico's abundant wildlife and scenic beauty.

Second Mesa, Arizona
Dinner on the Reservation

Dinner for Six to Eight
Melon Salsa with Blue Corn Chips
Southwestern Black Bean Soup
Indian Fry Bread Tacos
Mesa Summer Squash & Corn
Hopi Blue Corn Hotcakes
with Sweet Peaches

About your Destination

Arizona is a beautiful land filled with many wonders: magnificent desserts, ponderosa pine forests, mountain peaks and canyons. Historical roots running deeper than the canyons are witnessed with a visit to one of the reservations of the 14 Indian tribes who reside within the borders of Arizona. Each tribe is distinct, with a unique people and culture, but all are proudly united by their Indian heritage. Arizona's name comes from the Spanish interpretation of the Aztec Indian word "Arizuma," which means "silver- bearing," and is also based on the Pima Indian word "Arizonac," which means "little spring place."

The Hopi Indians make their home on a reservation in northern Arizona. This peaceful and close-knit tribe of Native Americans built Old Oraibi, which is believed to be the oldest continuously inhabited settlement in the U.S.,

continued

Melon Salsa with Blue Corn Chips

Makes approximately 3½ cups

Ingredients

1½ C. coarsely chopped
  honeydew melon
1½ C. coarsely chopped
  cantaloupe melon
1 jalapeño or serrano chile,
  finely chopped
¼ C. coarsely chopped fresh cilantro
2 T. lime juice
1 T. olive oil
Salt and pepper to taste
Blue corn chips*

Instructions

In a large bowl, combine both melons, jalapeño, cilantro, lime juice, and olive oil; mix thoroughly and season with salt and pepper. Refrigerate for 2 to 12 hours and serve with blue corn chips.

Blue corn chips are tortilla–style chips made with blue corn. They are sold by the bag and are available in most supermarkets.

continued from page 86
dating back as far as 1150 AD. The Hopi reservation is made up of 12 traditional villages on three mesas (flat mountains), which rise above low altitude deserts. In the past, mesas provided protection from invading Navajo and Apache Indians. The Hopi are a peaceful, but very private group of people. Many Native American tribes struggle to maintain a balance between the tourism, which highlights their culture and provides income, and living their traditional way of life without feeling violated. Respect other's customs and way of life when visiting.

Theme & Setting

The Hopi Indians are best known for their agricultural skills. Through terracing and irrigation, they have been able to grow corn, cotton, beans, squash, tobacco and more, all in the middle of the Arizona desert. Your Dinner on the Reservation features some traditional crops of the Hopi Indians, such as blue corn, but also celebrates a diversity of Native American dishes.

Set the scene with pieces of corn in the husk, dishes of dried beans and whole squash, arranged as a centerpiece. Arts of the Native Americans can also be displayed, includng dolls, woven baskets and tapestries, and wicker coil plaques. Traditional Indian flute music projects a quiet and peaceful dinner mood. Complete the evening with legends or other stories of Native Americans, shared around the table with dessert.

Southwestern Black Bean Soup

Makes 8 servings

Ingredients

2 T. vegetable oil
1 small onion, chopped
2 cloves garlic, minced
4 slices smoked bacon, chopped
Chipotle chile pepper in adobo
    sauce, to taste*
1 tsp. cumin seed, toasted
    and ground
2 carrots, diced
2 stalks celery, diced
1 red bell pepper, seeded, diced
1 bay leaf
4 C. chicken or vegetable stock
1 (15 oz.) can black beans, rinsed
    and drained
1 (14 oz.) can plum tomatoes
Salt and pepper to taste
Fresh cilantro, chopped, optional

Instructions

In a large pot, heat oil on high. Add onions and garlic and sauté for 4 to 5 minutes or until softened and golden. Add bacon and cook for 3 to 4 minutes or until lightly crisp. Add chile pepper, cumin, carrots, celery, red bell pepper, bay leaf and chicken stock; bring to a boil. Reduce heat to low and simmer for 25 minutes or until vegetables are tender. Remove and discard bay leaf. Add beans and tomatoes, cover and continue to cook for 10 to 15 minutes or until soup has thickened. Transfer one-third of soup to a food processor or blender and puree until smooth. Pour pureed mixture back into remaining soup, stir to blend and season with salt and pepper to taste. If desired, garnish with cilantro to serve.

Chipotle chiles, or peppers, in adobo sauce are smoked jalapeno peppers that have been canned in a special red seasoned sauce. They are generally available in supermarkets and sold in 7 ounce cans. Personal heat level preferences will help you determine how much to include in the dish.

Arizona Quick Facts

Date of Statehood:	February 14, 1912
Population:	5,130,632
Capital:	Phoenix
State Bird:	Cactus Wren
State Flower:	Saguaro Cactus Blossom
State Nickname:	The Grand Canyon State

Indian Fry Bread Tacos

Makes 8 servings

Ingredients for fry bread

5 C. whole wheat flour

1 T. baking powder

1 tsp. salt

¼ C. milk

2 C. warm water

2 C. oil or shortening for frying

Special equipment – deep-frying
thermometer, optional

Ingredients for tacos

1½ lbs. ground meat
(buffalo, beef, pork or venison)

1 C. diced onions

2 T. vegetable oil

8 rounds of fry bread

1 head lettuce, shredded

2 C. shredded sharp Cheddar
cheese

3 tomatoes, diced

1 (4 oz.) can diced green chiles

Instructions

To make fry bread: In a large bowl,
mix flour, baking powder and
salt. Stir in milk and water with
a wooden spoon, and then mix
with hands until well blended.
Add additional flour if mixture
is too sticky. Form dough into
a ball, cover and let stand a few
minutes. Divide dough into eight
equal portions. Roll first portion
into a small ball. Dust dough ball
lightly with flour and pat into
a flat circle. Then, quickly flip
flattened dough back and forth
between the palms of your hands
so it thins and spreads until it is
5″ to 6″ in diameter. Make a small
slit in the center of the dough
with a knife, to keep fry bread
flat while cooking. In a medium
saucepan, heat oil to 350°F, or
drop a pinch of dough into the oil;
oil is hot enough when it sizzles.
Carefully lay dough on top of oil.
When dough is lightly browned
and puffed up, turn over with a
long-handled fork. When second
side is lightly browned, remove to
a paper towel-lined plate; repeat
with remaining dough. **To make
tacos:** In a large skillet, cook meat
and onions in oil over medium-
high heat until browned. Divide
meat evenly over fry bread and top
with lettuce, cheese, tomatoes and
chiles to serve.

Mesa Summer Squash & Corn

Makes 6 to 8 servings

Ingredients

3 T. butter or margarine
½ C. chopped yellow onion
2 summer squash, julienned (yellow crookneck or zucchini)
3 cloves garlic, minced
1 (4 oz.) can chopped green chiles, drained
2 C. fresh corn kernels (or canned corn, drained)
2 tomatoes, seeded and coarsely chopped
½ tsp. chili powder
Salt and pepper to taste
¾ C. shredded Cheddar cheese

Instructions

In a large skillet, melt butter over medium heat and cook onion for 3 minutes or until soft. Add summer squash and garlic; cook for 5 minutes or until squash is crisp-tender. Add green chiles, corn, tomatoes and chili powder and cook for 3 minutes until heated through. Add salt and pepper to taste and transfer to a serving bowl; sprinkle with cheese and cover until melted.

Hopi Blue Corn Hotcakes with Sweet Peaches

Makes 6 to 8 dessert hotcakes

Ingredients

⅓ C. quick oats
⅓ C. flour
⅓ C. blue cornmeal*
2 T. brown sugar
1 tsp. baking powder
½ tsp. baking soda
¼ tsp. salt
2 large eggs, separated
1 C. buttermilk
Vegetable oil for cooking
4 ripe peaches, peeled and diced
Sugar to taste
Whipped cream, optional

Instructions

In a large bowl, combine oats, flour, cornmeal, brown sugar, baking powder, baking soda and salt. In a separate bowl, slightly beat eggs yolks. Slowly add yolks and buttermilk to dry ingredients and stir just until moist. In a separate bowl, beat egg whites until stiff, then fold into batter. Heat a large skillet or griddle and brush lightly with oil. Spoon batter onto hot surface, using about ⅓ cup per hotcake. When bubbles form on surface and begin to pop, turn hotcake to cook the other side. Serve with diced peaches sweetened with sugar to taste; add a dollop of whipped cream if desired.

If blue cornmeal is unavailable, substitute yellow cornmeal.

Food for Thought

• Agriculture has been a way of life for the Hopis for centuries; it continues to be of great importance today. For hundreds of years, blue corn has been a Hopi preference and is still cultivated today. Other historic crops included squash, beans and sunflowers. Over the years, Spaniards introduced additional crops such as peaches, watermelons and chilies. Today, Hopis also cultivate carrots, onions and peas.

• The grazing of cattle provides an excellent source of meat.

• Wild plants are used as staple foods or to season vegetables and meat. Beeweed, wild potatoes, pinyon nuts, yucca fruits, tangy mustard and wormwood name a few.

While in the Area

• Experience a visit to the Grand Canyon, one of the most recognizable natural wonders in the United States. Located in the northern part of Arizona, the Colorado River flows though the longest gorge in the world. It is 290 miles long, measures up to 18 miles across from rim to rim and has an average depth of one mile.

• Stay the night at the Hopi Cultural Center, which houses a small hotel, restaurant and museum. Enjoy the beautiful Hopi arts of wicker coil plaques, pottery, wood carving, sterling jewelry and weavings of native cotton. The most unique artwork is seen in the Kachina "dolls," which are actually stylized religious icons, meticulously carved from cottonwood root and painted to represent figures from Hopi mythology.

• With a Hopi guide, visit Awatovi, an abandoned Hopi settlement, to see the ruins of a 500-year-old pueblo and a 17th century Spanish mission. Multi-level adobe homes housed clans of Hopi Indians.

Big Island, Hawaii
'Ono 'Ailana Luau (Delicious Island Feast)

Buffet Dinner for Six to Twelve
Blush Fruit Punch
Hawaiian Fruit Salad
Macadamia Nut-Crusted Mahi Mahi
Slow Cooker Kalua Pig – Pulled Pork
Aloha Sweet Potatoes
Banana Macadamia Cakes *with*
White Chocolate Sauce

About your Destination

Hawaii is the home of many peoples and many islands. With no ethnic majority, Hawaii represents the American Melting Pot, with Japanese-Americans, Filipino-Americans, Chinese-Americans, European, Native Polynesian descendents and others.

Hawaii is the only state comprised completely of islands. The Hawaiian Archipelago consists of well over 100 scattered points of land, spanning more than 1,200 miles of the Pacific Ocean. The main Islands are, Niihau, Kauai, Oahu, Molokai, Kohoolawe, Lanai, Maui, and Hawaii, also known as the Big Island. Private ownership of Niihau and off-limit status of government-owned Kohoolawe, make them unique.

Blush Fruit Punch

Makes 12 servings

Ingredients

1½ qts. orange juice, chilled

1 qt. pineapple juice, chilled

1 liter lemon-lime soda, chilled

¾ C. grenadine syrup

Assorted fruit slices, such as strawberries, bananas or pineapple, optional

Frozen fruit juice cubes, optional

Instructions

In a large punch bowl, stir together orange juice, pineapple juice, soda and grenadine. If desired, garnish with sliced fruit or frozen juice cubes to serve.

Theme & Setting

The origin of the luau is rooted in royalty and religious history. In the year 1819, King Kamehameha II held a great luau feast as a symbolic end to the practice of separate dining for men of importance versus commoners and women. Over the years, large and elaborate luaus have been held to mark the birthdays and coronations of kings. The hula and Polynesian fire knife dancing became common luau entertainment. Today, luaus are often held to celebrate important milestones such as a first birthday or high school graduation.

Suggestions for natural décor include grass table skirting for the buffet, bamboo placemats and tropical flower arrangements of orchids, hibiscus, bird of paradise or other exotic flowers. Decorate with additional tropical plants and fresh coconuts and pineapples. If partying outdoors, tiki torches add ambiance; tropical fabrics dress up an indoor luau location. Invite guests to dress within the theme, wearing colorful Hawaiian print shirts, straw hats, grass skirts, etc. And, of course, greet them with a kiss and a flower lei. Finally, enjoy Polynesian music, hula dancing or simply visiting around a fire pit.

Hawaiian Fruit Salad

Makes 6 servings

Ingredients

1 whole fresh pineapple

1 (15 oz.) can mandarin oranges, drained

1½ C. sliced fresh strawberries

1½ C. green grapes, halved

½ C. sweetened flaked coconut, toasted, divided

1¼ C. pina colada- or vanilla-flavored yogurt

¼ tsp. coconut or vanilla extract, optional

Kale or other decorative lettuce leaves, optional

Instructions

To carve a pineapple bowl, stand pineapple upright and vertically cut one-third from one side, leaving leaves attached. Set smaller piece aside. Remove strips of pineapple flesh from the large section, leaving a ½″ thick shell; discard core. Cut strips into bite-sized chunks. Invert shell on paper towels to drain. From the reserved piece of pineapple, cut fruit into bite-sized chunks; discard skin. In a large bowl, combine fruits and ¼ cup coconut; set aside. If desired, add extract to yogurt and stir to blend. Fold yogurt into fruit. If desired, garnish a serving tray or shallow bowl with lettuce leaves; set pineapple bowl on top. Fill with fruit salad and sprinkle with remaining ¼ cup coconut.

Macadamia Nut-Crusted Mahi Mahi

Makes 8 servings

Ingredients

10 oz. coarsely ground, roasted macadamia nuts

1 C. panko*

¼ C. flour

½ C. butter, melted

Vegetable oil, for brushing foil

8 (6 to 8 oz.) mahi mahi fillets

Salt and pepper to taste

¼ C. coconut milk

Instructions

Preheat oven to 425°F. In a medium bowl, stir together nuts, panko, flour and butter; set aside. Line a baking sheet with aluminum foil and brush generously with oil. Place mahi mahi on the foil and season with salt and pepper on both sides. Bake for 5 minutes. Remove from oven, brush top sides with coconut milk and pat with nut mixture to form a crust. Return to the oven; bake for 5 to 10 minutes or until crust is golden brown. Allow to stand 10 minutes before serving.

Panko is a Japanese light, crisp and coarse breadcrumb, used to make a deliciously crunchy crust.

Slow Cooker Kalua Pig – Pulled Pork

Kalua pig, also called Kalua pork, is a very common Hawaiian food, and the centerpiece of a luau. The pig is roasted in an outdoor oven, called an "imu," which has been dug into the ground. The same wonderful smoky, salty flavor of true Kalua pork is created with this much easier slow cooker version.

Makes 12 servings

Ingredients

1 (6 lb.) pork butt roast
1½ T. Hawaiian sea salt*
1 T. liquid smoke flavoring

Instructions

With a carving fork, pierce roast all over. Rub salt over the roast, then rub liquid smoke over the roast. Place roast in slow cooker; cover and cook on low for 16 to 20 hours, turning once. Remove from slow cooker, shred and add drippings as needed to moisten.

*Hawaiian sea salt is also called alaea, alae and Hawaiian red salt. It is pink in color due to a natural mineral called "alaea" (volcanic baked red clay) which enriches the salt with iron oxide. It comes in fine and coarse textures and is found in gourmet shops. Standard sea salt can be used as a substitute.

Aloha Sweet Potatoes

Makes 8 servings

Ingredients

4 to 5 medium sweet potatoes
½ C. butter
1 C. brown sugar
½ C. water
¼ C. sweetened flaked coconut

Instructions

In a large pot over medium-high heat, boil sweet potatoes in their skins for 25 minutes or just until fork-tender. When cool enough to handle, peel and cut into 1½" slices. In a large skillet, melt butter over medium heat. Stir in brown sugar and water; cook for 5 minutes. Reduce heat to low and add sweet potatoes. Cook, tossing lightly until sweet potatoes are glazed and warmed through. Sprinkle with coconut before serving.

Hawaii Quick Facts

Date of Statehood:	August 21, 1959
Population:	1,211,537
Capital:	Honolulu
State Bird:	Nene (Hawaiian Goose)
State Flower:	Yellow Hibiscus
State Nickname:	Aloha State

Banana & Macadamia Cakes with White Chocolate Sauce

Makes 12 servings

Ingredients for cakes

1½ C. flour
1½ tsp. baking soda
¼ tsp. salt
⅛ tsp. ground nutmeg
1¼ C. mashed ripe bananas (about 3 large)
½ C. sugar
¼ C. dark brown sugar
½ C. unsalted butter, melted
¼ C. milk
1 large egg
1 C. unsalted macadamia nuts, toasted and chopped, divided

Ingredients for sauce

8 oz. premium white chocolate baking squares or chips
1 C. heavy whipping cream
2 T. sugar
2 T. unsalted butter

Instructions

To make cakes: Preheat oven to 350°F. Grease 12 muffin cups. Sift flour, baking soda, salt and nutmeg into a large bowl. In a medium bowl, combine bananas, both sugars, butter, milk and egg. Fold banana mixture into dry ingredients; then fold in ½ cup nuts. Divide batter among prepared cake cups. Sprinkle remaining ½ cup nuts over tops of muffins. Bake for 25 minutes or until golden brown and a wooden toothpick inserted into center comes out clean. **To make sauce:** Chop chocolate into small pieces. In a small saucepan over medium heat, combine cream and sugar. While stirring, bring mixture almost to a boil; remove from heat. Add chocolate and butter; stir until smooth and chocolate has melted. Spoon warm sauce over warm cakes to serve.

Note: _Sauce may be refrigerated for later use; reheat in a double boiler. The cakes and sauce work independently as well. Serve un-sauced cakes as breakfast muffins or use this sauce to complement other desserts. Make a substitution of bittersweet chocolate for a different taste._

Food for Thought

- Immigrants from China, Japan, Puerto Rico, the Philippines and elsewhere brought their unique dishes, blended them with the Native Hawaiian/Polynesian cuisine, and a fusion was born. Hawaiian cuisine blends fresh ingredients, exotic flavors, rich traditions and diverse ethnic influences.

- Macadamia nuts originated in Australia and found their way to Hawaii in the late 1800s. The nuts quickly grew in popularity and production rate to make Hawaii the macadamia nut capital of the world, producing over 90 percent of the world's supply.

- Pineapples are a familiar symbol of Hawaii. In the 1960s, Hawaii was responsible for 80 percent of the world's pineapple, but production declined dramatically in recent years due to cheaper production elsewhere. Today, commercial exports are small, but you can still bring back a delicious fresh pineapple from your Hawaiian vacation.

- Sugarcane, coffee and taro are all crops in Hawaii. Poi, the traditional staple food in Hawaii, is produced by mashing cooked taro.

- Spam is considered a delicacy and a comfort food in Hawaii, where it is so popular that it is even served at large fast food chains. A convenience store version called *musabi* is also available; a slice of Spam and a patty of rice are wrapped in seaweed.

While in the Area

- Explore Puukohola Heiau, the largest restored ancient Hawaiian religious temple. Built on the Big Island by King Kamehameha I in 1790, it's now a national historic site, featuring John Young's homestead as well. Young, a stranded British sailor, served as an advisor to the king, handling his business affairs with foreign traders and helping him extend his reign over the Hawaiian Islands.

- Play in the snow atop Big Island's Mauna Kea, the world's tallest mountain (measured from the ocean floor). This dormant volcano hosts the world's largest astronomical observatory, with telescopes operated by astronomers from eleven countries. This is a great location because of the extremely dry and cloud-free atmosphere.

- Watch hot lava flow when you visit Hawaii Volcanoes National Park. The park's Crater Rim Drive is an 11-mile road encircling the summit of the caldera (large crater formed by volcanic action), passing through a lush forest, traversing the caldera floor and providing scenic stops and short walking trails.

Sonoma, California
Hors d'oeuvres Alfresco

Cocktail Party for Six to Eight
Grape Sparklers
Marinated Feta with Capers
Walnut & Port Wine Cheese Apples
Slow Cooker Marinated Mushrooms
Italian Shrimp Skewers
Sonoma Stuffed Dates
Tomato & Olive Bruschetta
Wine-Poached Pears *with*
Chocolate Drizzle

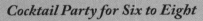

About your Destination

The quaint town of Sonoma lies in a picturesque valley of Northern California where fertile land, mineral springs, creeks, abundant game and adobe soil for building material made it the perfect site for missionary Jose Altimira to begin his work. Spanish and Mexican influences can be seen firsthand with a visit to the original Mission San Francisco Solano de Sonoma. Sweeping vineyard views are enjoyed throughout Sonoma County, especially from the local wineries which bottle world-class wines. A passion for the arts is displayed with sculpture gardens, live

continued

Grape Sparklers

Makes 8 drinks

Ingredients

4 lbs. red grapes, stemmed, divided

1 (750 ml.) bottle dry sparkling wine, chilled

8 mint sprigs, optional

Instructions

Thinly slice 1 cup grapes and set aside in refrigerator. In a food processor, coarsely chop remaining grapes. In a medium saucepan over medium heat, simmer chopped grapes for 5 minutes or until grapes have released most of their juice. Working in batches, strain grape juice into a bowl, pressing hard on the solids. Refrigerate until cold. Divide sliced grapes equally between eight wine or champagne glasses; then divide the fresh grape juice between the glasses. Finally, top each glass with sparkling wine and, if desired, garnish with mint sprigs.

continued from page 98
performances and high-end galleries throughout the area. Near perfect weather makes recreation and dining alfresco popular. Culinary arts are important in California Wine Country, where Spanish and Italian influences are enjoyed along with international trends, due to the nearby renowned culinary school in Napa Valley.

Theme & Setting

Sophisticated country charm welcomes you to an alfresco party in Sonoma, California. Creating a Wine Country scene begins by loosely arranging fresh garden flowers in a vase, lighting outdoor candles, and decorating with natural greens, creams and pale pink shades. Paper lanterns will also set a casual, romantic mood. Set up a self-serve buffet, decorated with grapes and wine bottles. The ambiance will almost be complete when you play recorded Spanish guitar music. The final touch is the good friends, great food and relaxed fun you will have when you sit back with a drink and hors d'oeuvres. Welcome to Sonoma.

Marinated Feta with Capers

Makes 6 servings

Ingredients

12 oz. feta cheese, not crumbled
½ tsp. mixed peppercorns
8 coriander seeds
1 bay leaf
2 cloves garlic, sliced
2 T. drained capers
Fresh oregano or thyme sprigs
Olive oil, to cover
Frill picks

Instructions

Cut feta into ½″ to ¾″ cubes. Coarsely crush or grind peppercorns and coriander seeds. Pack feta cubes and bay leaf into a large glass jar, interspersing layers of cheese with garlic, crushed peppercorns and coriander, capers and fresh oregano or thyme sprigs. Add enough olive oil to cover the cheese. Seal jar and marinate in the refrigerator for 1 to 2 weeks. Serve with frill picks.

Walnut & Port Wine Cheese Apples

Makes 24 pieces

Ingredients

2 large apples
2 T. lemon juice
2 C. water
4 oz. port wine cheese*, room temperature
1¼ C. chopped walnuts

Instructions

Core and slice each apple into 12 wedges. In a medium bowl, combine lemon juice and water; dip apples to prevent browning and place on paper towels. Holding apple slice by one end, use paper towels to dry the other half of the slice. Dip dry half of apple into softened port wine cheese to coat. Dip cheese-coated end of apple into walnuts to coat, pressing gently. Fan apple slices around a tray to serve as finger food.

*Port wine cheese is sold with cheese spreads in the cold case of most supermarkets.

California Quick Facts

Date of Statehood:	September 9, 1850
Population:	33,871,648
Capital:	Sacramento
State Bird:	California Valley Quail
State Flower:	California Poppy
State Nickname:	Golden State

Slow Cooker Marinated Mushrooms

Makes 6 to 8 appetizer servings

Ingredients

2 (8 oz.) pkgs. whole fresh
    mushrooms
½ C. butter (no substitutions)
1 (1 oz.) env. ranch dressing mix*
Frill picks

Instructions

Place all ingredients in a slow
cooker. Cook on high temperature
setting, stirring occasionally to coat
mushrooms, for 2 hours or until
mushrooms darken and are tender.
Adjust temperature to low setting
and serve with frill picks.

*Use Italian dressing mix as an
alternative flavor.*

Italian Shrimp Skewers

Makes 8 servings

Ingredients

2 lbs. jumbo shrimp, peeled,
    deveined
¼ C. olive oil
3 T. vegetable oil
1¼ C. extra fine dry bread crumbs
1 clove garlic, crushed
1 T. chopped fresh parsley
Salt and pepper to taste
8 wooden skewers, soaked in water
    for 30 minutes
Lemon wedges

Instructions

Rinse shrimp in cold water and pat
dry with paper towels. In a large
bowl, combine oils and shrimp,
tossing to coat evenly. Add bread
crumbs, garlic and parsley; season
with salt and pepper to taste. Toss
shrimp with bread crumbs to coat
evenly. Cover and refrigerate for
1 hour. Preheat grill or broiler.
Thread shrimp onto skewers. Cook
over medium to medium-high
heat for 2 minutes on each side or
until bread crumbs are golden and
shrimp is cooked through. Serve
with lemon wedges.

Sonoma Stuffed Dates

*Don't let the dates scare you, as the
combination of bacon and nut flavors
combine with the sweet goodness of
the date to surprise even the skeptic.*

Makes 18 pieces

Ingredients

18 whole pitted dates
18 whole blanched almonds
6 slices bacon

Instructions

Preheat oven to 400°F. Stuff each
date with one whole almond. Cut
bacon slices into thirds and wrap
one piece around each date. Place
dates on a baking sheet with the
seam side of the bacon down. Bake
for 20 to 25 minutes or until bacon
is lightly crisp. Drain on a paper
towel and serve warm.

Note: *Dates may be stuffed and
wrapped ahead; store in the freezer.*

Tomato & Olive Bruschetta

Makes 8 servings

Ingredients

1 loaf day-old Italian bread, cut into ½″ thick slices

1 tsp. extra-virgin olive oil

½ medium red onion, thinly sliced

⅓ C. kalamata or Niçise olives, pitted and chopped

⅓ C. chopped yellow bell pepper

2 C. cherry or grape tomatoes, halved

Salt and pepper to taste

Fresh cilantro or Italian parsley leaves, optional

Instructions

Broil bread slices for 1 minute on each side or until lightly toasted; set aside. In a medium skillet over medium-low heat, heat oil; cook onion for 10 minutes or until lightly browned. Transfer to a medium bowl and add olives and yellow bell pepper. Return skillet to heat, add tomatoes and sear briefly, until just heated through. Add tomatoes to onion mixture and toss gently. Serve with toasted bread (bruschetta), season with salt and pepper and if desired, garnish with fresh herbs.

Wine-Poached Pears with Chocolate Drizzle

Makes 6 servings

Ingredients

1 (750 ml.) bottle red wine

⅔ C. sugar

2¼ C. water

¼ C. lemon juice

2 T. lemon zest

½ tsp. ground ginger

½ tsp. ground nutmeg

½ tsp. ground cinnamon

Pinch of ground cloves

6 fresh whole California pears, peeled*

¾ C. fat-free chocolate syrup, warmed, optional

Instructions

In a large stock pot, make a simple syrup by combining wine, sugar, water, lemon juice and lemon zest. Bring to a boil and continue to boil until reduced by one-fourth. Reduce heat to low and stir in ginger, nutmeg, cinnamon and cloves. Stand pears in pan with syrup (not touching each other); cover and simmer for 15 minutes. Remove pan from heat and allow pears to cool slightly in syrup. With a slotted spoon, gently lift pears from syrup to a platter or bowl. Plate each pear to an individual serving dish and drizzle with 3 tablespoons warm poaching syrup and 2 tablespoons warm chocolate sauce to serve.

Note: Pears can be poached several days in advance and refrigerated. Warm in the microwave or serve cold.

*Bosc is the traditional variety used in this dish, but any variety may be used.

California growers harvest Bosc, Seckel, Comice and Red pears, along with the more common Bartlett pears. Ranking number one in Bartlett production, California produces 50% of the U.S. crop each year. Pears do not ripen on trees, so they are picked while still green, but mature.

Food for Thought

- In the early days of California history, vineyards and wheat fields were planted by the Franciscan Priests and their native converts to supply Holy Communion wine and bread.

- Wine bottling is a critical culinary art form in Sonoma Valley, where a variety of excellent Pinot Noir, Chardonnay, Merlot, Cabernet Sauvignon and Zinfandel wines are produced. In Sonoma County, not only is wine an art, but the wine labels are considered to be "art" as well; visit the world's largest art gallery devoted exclusively to wine labels.

- Small scale gourmet olive oil production is important in Sonoma, where local olive growers are gaining worldwide recognition. You will understand why when you taste the oil for yourself.

While in the Area

- Shop at the farmers markets and antique shops of Sonoma. You can meet the local farmers and even find pick-your-own farms where you can select the freshest flowers, plumpest pumpkins, and mouthwatering apples and berries of your choice. Take home a unique piece of history when you find a treasure in one of the many antique shops where you are welcome to browse for a piece of the past.

- Attend the annual Mustard Festival in nearby Napa Valley. Created to invite visitors to witness the dazzling hues of green and gold covering the fields of Wine Country during the winter months of January, February and March, the Mustard Festival kicks off two months of lavish parties, dinners, art shows, concerts, auctions and wine tastings.

- Ride the train and touch the animals at the petting zoo when you visit Train Town. This small amusement-style park is home to a brilliant scale train and railroad replica. This fun stop is for kids of any age.

Cody, Wyoming
Cookie's Cowboy Chuckwagon

Cookout for Eight to Ten
Spiced Peach Salad
Chuckwagon Wheel Pasta Salad
Baked BBQ Chicken Wings
Savory Beef Brisket
Cookie's Roasted Potatoes
Raisin Bread Pudding
Cowboy Coffee

About Your Destination

Cody, just east of Yellowstone National Park, is a small Wyoming town offering a big Western welcome to visitors. The town's namesake is Colonel William F. Cody. The title of Colonel was earned through his Army career that spanned a number of years, but the more recognized name of Buffalo Bill was earned through his notorious buffalo hunting. Cody's experiences were varied, from rugged activities like cattle herding, working wagon trains, riding Pony Express, fur trading and gold mining to more cultured activities of acting and entertaining. He is most widely known for his Wild West show which toured throughout the country and provided roles for entertainers like sharpshooter Annie Oakley and "Wild Bill" Hickock.

continued

Spiced Peach Salad

Canned peaches are this dishes only true connection to the chuckwagon meal. However, this cool sweet treat will accompany the other tastes of the West quite nicely.

Makes 8 to 10 servings

Ingredients

½ C. sugar
3 T. vinegar
2 C. water
1 T. whole cloves
4 cinnamon sticks
1 (6 oz.) pkg. peach gelatin
1 (29 oz.) can peach slices

Instructions

In a medium saucepan, combine sugar, vinegar and water. Tie cloves and cinnamon in a cheesecloth bag; add it to the saucepan. Bring mixture to a boil; reduce heat and simmer for 10 minutes. Remove from heat and discard spice bag. Add gelatin and stir until dissolved. Drain peaches, reserving syrup; set peaches aside. Add water to reserved syrup to equal 2 cups of liquid; stir into gelatin mixture. Chill until slightly thickened, then add peaches. Transfer to a 2-quart glass bowl and chill until firm.

continued from page 104

The Colonel first entered the Big Horn Basin of Wyoming in the 1870s while serving as a guide for a Yale geologist. The lands, rich with opportunities and resources, drew him back during the mid-1890s, when he and others worked to build a strong business community. Today, the town of Cody welcomes visitors, offering unique Western entertainment and history lessons.

Theme & Setting

Cookie is calling... "Come 'n' get it!" Cattle drives work up big appetites requiring home-cookin' that sticks to the ribs. Cookie is the moniker given to the person cookin' the grub for the cowhands. Meals were prepared out of the back of a chuckwagon, over an open fire. Evening entertainment might include cowboy poetry and songs, as these men were more sensitive than they let on. Pocket harmonicas were popular on the open range.

Call up some cowboys and cowgirls of your own, and be sure to share the chuckwagon rules. Here is a short list to get you started:

- No one eats until Cookie calls.
- It's okay to eat with your fingers; the food is clean.
- Don't take the last helping unless you are the last to get your food.
- When you mount your horse to leave, ride downwind from the wagon.
- Strangers are always welcome at the wagon.

Decorate with bandanas, ropes/lassos, cowboy hats and cactus plants. Other "Western" decoration ideas include a homemade saloon sign, wanted posters and hay bales (if outdoors). Invite guests to dress in themed clothing. Following dinner, gather 'round a campfire, firepit or fireplace and share some cowboy poetry or music of your own.

Chuckwagon Wheel Pasta Salad

Makes 10 servings

Ingredients

¼ C. cider vinegar

1 T. cooking oil

⅓ C. mayonnaise

2 T. thick & chunky salsa

Dash of hot pepper sauce

¼ tsp. salt

½ tsp. ground black pepper

8 oz. rotelle (wagon wheel) pasta, cooked, rinsed and drained

¼ C. chopped celery

¼ C. chopped green bell peppers

2 T. chopped green onions

¼ C. green olives, sliced

½ C. black olives, sliced

½ C. frozen corn, cooked

½ C. black-eyed peas, rinsed and drained

Instructions

In a large bowl, whisk first seven ingredients. Add pasta and remaining ingredients; stir until evenly coated. Refrigerate overnight; stir before serving.

Baked BBQ Chicken Wings

Makes 8 to 10 appetizer servings

Ingredients

2½ lbs. chicken wings

4 to 6 T. cooking oil, divided

1 (18 oz.) bottle BBQ sauce (Bulls-Eye recommended)

½ C. brown sugar

1 T. molasses

¼ C. apricot jam

5 dashes of Worcestershire sauce

Instructions

In a large skillet, working in batches, brown wings in small amount of oil. Set aside on paper towel-lined plates to drain. When batch cooking is complete, place wings in a single layer in a roasting pan. Preheat oven to 350°F. In a bowl, whisk together remaining ingredients and pour over chicken. Cover with foil and cook for 30 minutes; reduce heat and remove foil to cook for an additional 10 to 15 minutes or until browned and cooked through.

Wyoming Quick Facts

Date of Statehood:	July 10, 1890
Population:	493,782
Capital:	Cheyenne
State Bird:	Western Meadowlark
State Flower:	Indian Paintbrush
State Nickname:	Equality State

Savory Beef Brisket

Makes 8 to 10 servings

Ingredients

1 small (4 to 5 lb.) beef brisket
½ C. water
1 T. flour
½ tsp. garlic salt
½ tsp. pepper
1 yellow onion, sliced into rings

Instructions

Prepare grill or fire for cooking at a low temperature. Using a very large sheet of heavy-duty foil, make a pouch large enough to hold the brisket while leaving room to fold and seal. Lightly grease the inside of the pouch. In a small bowl, whisk together water and flour; pour into pouch. Sprinkle brisket with garlic salt and pepper; add to the pouch. Arrange onion on top of the brisket. Triple-fold opening of the pouch to seal. Cook on grill or campfire grate for 2 hours, turning every 30 minutes until desired tenderness is reached.

Note: To prepare brisket in the oven, place seasoned brisket and onion in a roasting pan and bake at 350°F for 1 hour, uncovered. Add ½ cup water (no flour) and enough extra water or beef broth to yield about ½˝ of liquid in the roasting pan; reduce temperature to 300°F, cover pan tightly and continue to cook for 3 hours or until fork-tender.

Cookie's Roasted Potatoes

Makes 8 to 10 servings

Ingredients

5 lbs. red potatoes, cut in ¾˝ pieces
1 large onion, chopped
6 cloves garlic, chopped
1½ C. chopped par-cooked bacon
1½ C. butter, melted
Salt and pepper to taste
1 C. shredded smoked cheese*
½ C. chopped chives

Instructions

Preheat oven to 400°F. In a roasting pan, combine first five ingredients; stir until evenly coated. Cover with foil and cook for 1 hour or until potatoes are almost fork-tender. Remove foil, season with salt and pepper, and cook for 20 minutes or until potatoes are golden brown. Sprinkle with cheese and chives; serve when cheese is melted.

Note: To cook on the grill or campfire grate, slice potatoes and onions into smaller pieces and divide mixture between 3 or 4 packets. Use purchased foil pouches or make them with heavy-duty foil. Do not fill pouches completely full; allow air to circulate with a "tent" shape. Seal tightly to prevent butter from escaping. Cook for 20 to 30 minutes or until potatoes are tender.

*Smoked cheese adds a cookout taste to your oven-roasted potatoes; try Smoked Cheddar, Smoked Pepper Jack or Smoked Gouda.

Raisin Bread Pudding

Makes 6 to 8 servings

Ingredients

1 large loaf raisin bread (sliced)
½ C. butter
½ C. brown sugar
Ground nutmeg to taste
Ground cinnamon to taste
1 C. chopped walnuts
4 apples, cored, peeled and chopped
3 large eggs
4 C. milk
Whipped cream, optional

Instructions

Preheat oven to 325°F and grease a 9 x 13″ baking dish. Butter each side of raisin bread slices; cut into cubes. In a large bowl, toss bread cubes with brown sugar and nutmeg and cinnamon to taste. Spread bread mixture evenly in prepared baking dish. Sprinkle walnuts and apples over bread mixture. In a large bowl, beat eggs with milk and pour over top of the walnuts and apples. Bake for 1 hour or until golden brown and puffed up. If desired, serve with whipped cream.

**Note:** This recipe can be prepared in a Dutch oven over a fire. Line a 10″ Dutch oven kettle with foil for easier cleanup. Cut apples in tiny pieces and add 1 additional egg to mixture. Bake for about 1 hour.

Cowboy Coffee

Strong black coffee has long been a cowboy staple. A kettle of cold mountain water is boiled over the campfire, ground coffee is thrown in and the resulting brew is enjoyed unfiltered. Sometimes an egg shell was crushed and added to the pot to help settle the grounds and add calcium. While not a sophisticated way to brew coffee, it works well after a long day of roping and wrangling.

Food for Thought

- Genuine chuckwagon food was prepared with the simplest of ingredients; cornmeal, flour and dry beans were staples. Foods were preserved with brine, salt, pickling or dehydration. A good supply of beef was available, and cowboys ate off the land as well, including rabbit, venison, wild berries, etc.

- As time went on, the addition of canned goods like milk, peaches and tomatoes were added to the list of available ingredients for chuckwagon cooking. Fresh milk was not available, as the cattle being herded were beef cattle, not dairy cattle.

- "Chuckwagon" feasts are still prepared by "Cookies." Cowboys still work on ranches, chuckwagon cooking contests are held throughout the West and visitors seek a new experiences on working ranches. A western dude ranch vacation can not only offer adventure, but amazing meals prepared by creative chefs.

While in the Area

- Visit Yellowstone, the oldest national park of the United States, established in 1872. The park is so big that it is located in Wyoming, Montana and Idaho. While there, you may see grizzly bears, wolves, bison and elk. Old Faithful, other extraordinary geysers and hot springs are unique features of the park.

- Watch the Cody Night Rodeo. From June 1st through August 31st, you can witness the original American sport that has earned Cody the title of Rodeo Capital of the World.

- Saunter down the Old Town Trail to enjoy a collection of historic buildings and Western artifacts which provide a hands-on learning experience about Wyoming's frontier history. Placed on the original Cody town site, most of the collection comes from within 150 miles.

Seattle, Washington
"The Arts" – Culinary & Classic

Luncheon for Four
Spring French Baguette
Oyster Stew of the Northwest
Salmon Citrus Salad
Sautéed Apple Crêpes
Coffee with Chocolate Caramel Syrup

Another Taste of Washington
Chicken with Berry Sauce

About your Destination

The area of Seattle was first discovered by
Europeans in 1792, but the establishment of
the city began about 60 years later with the
development of the waterfront. Businesses
were established along the piers as commerce
and trade began to grow. In 1889, the "Great
Fire" destroyed the waterfront and 50 blocks
of downtown Seattle, but the city was quickly
rebuilt. Less than 10 years later, the gold rush up
north made Seattle the "Gateway to Alaska."

Seattle lies in the heart of Puget Sound, a body
of water which reaches inland as far as 50
miles from the Pacific Ocean. The waterways
are a complex system of channels and inlets
which meet up with the freshwater streams and
rivers pouring into the ocean's saltwater. The

continued

Spring French Baguette

Makes 4 servings

Ingredients

4 green onions, finely chopped
¼ C. chopped fresh cilantro
½ C. butter, softened
1½ tsp. lime zest
1 tsp. lime juice
½ tsp. minced garlic
1 (12″ to 15″) baguette
    or crusty French loaf

Instructions

In a medium bowl, cream together first six ingredients. Slice bread loaf from the top, leaving attached at the base. Spread desired amount of lime butter on each slice. Wrap loaf in foil and heat in the oven for 10 to 15 minutes, until heated through. Present loaf on cutting board to serve.

continued from page 110
famous salmon of the Northwest travel the route from the mountain streams to the Pacific Ocean. Their incredible journey leads them to the Alaskan waters and back, as they return to swim their way upstream to their Washington birthplace. Once there, they lay eggs before they die and the cycle of life begins again. A visit to the Puget Sound area provides opportunities for sightseeing, kayaking and hiking, as well as dining, shopping and cultural experiences.

Theme & Setting

Seattle is filled with opportunities to experience the arts. The Pacific Northwest Ballet is one of the country's leading companies and numerous theatrical productions are held in Seattle. The Seattle Art Museum is first-class and holds a very visible position in the city. Three main locations make up the museum: SAM Downtown, the Seattle Asian Art Museum that is housed in an historical building in Volunteer Park, and the nine-acre outdoor Olympic Sculpture Park at home along the waterfront.

Enjoy this luncheon as a prelude, postlude, or even interlude to experiencing the arts of your choosing. Invite friends to visit a local art museum or attend a theatrical production, dance recital, musical event or gallery opening. Class and elegance are the keys to your party. Serve the lunch on your finest china and use a dramatic monochromatic floral arrangement to adorn the table. Casual is often fun, but so is dressing up and pulling out all the stops!

Oyster Stew of the Northwest

Along the Northwest coastline, fresh oysters will perfect this dish; however, try a jar of oysters if you live where fresh are difficult to obtain.

Makes 4 servings

Ingredients

1 (10 oz.) jar Pacific oysters
1¼ C. water
1 T. finely chopped onion
3 T. butter
2 T. flour
¼ tsp. dried celery flakes
1 tsp. salt
⅛ tsp. garlic powder
Ground black pepper to taste
¼ tsp. Worcestershire sauce
¼ tsp. dried parsley flakes
1 C. milk
1 C. half & half

Instructions

Drain and thoroughly rinse oysters in a colander. In a small saucepan, combine oysters, water and onion. Bring to a boil, reduce heat and simmer for 3 minutes. Remove oysters and retain broth. Slice oysters into small pieces. In a medium to large pot, melt butter and sauté oysters over medium heat for 2 minutes. Slide oysters to one side of the pan; stir flour into butter on the other side of pan. Allow to gently bubble, while stirring, for 1 minute before gradually whisking in retained oyster broth and stirring with oysters. Add celery flakes, salt, garlic powder, pepper, Worcestershire sauce and parsley flakes; cook over medium heat, stirring occasionally, until thick. Stir in milk and half & half; cook until heated through. DO NOT BOIL!

Salmon Citrus Salad

Makes 4 servings

Ingredients for salmon

½ C. raspberry vinegar
¼ C. soy sauce
2 T. minced fresh cilantro
2 T. minced fresh gingerroot
1 T. olive oil
½ tsp. hot pepper sauce
⅛ tsp. ground black pepper
4 (6 oz.) salmon fillets

Ingredients for salsa

¾ C. pink grapefruit segments, cut into bite-sized pieces
½ C. orange segments, cut into bite-sized pieces

Washington Quick Facts

Date of Statehood:	November 11, 1889
Population:	5,894,121
Capital:	Olympia
State Bird:	Willow Goldfinch
State Flower:	Pink Rhododendron
State Nickname:	The Evergreen State

1 T. raspberry vinegar
1 T. honey
1 tsp. minced fresh cilantro
1 tsp. minced fresh gingerroot
⅛ tsp. hot pepper sauce

Ingredients for dressing & salad

2 T. raspberry vinegar
2 T. olive oil
½ tsp. sugar
¼ tsp. Dijon mustard
Nonstick cooking spray
1 lb. fresh lettuce greens

Instructions

To make salmon: In a large sealable plastic bag, combine first seven ingredients for salmon; seal and gently work ingredients together. Add salmon, seal and turn to coat; refrigerate for 2 hours.

To make salsa: In a medium bowl, combine salsa ingredients; cover and chill until just before serving.

To make salad dressing: In a jar with a tight-fitting lid, combine vinegar, oil, sugar and mustard; cover tightly, shake to blend.

To make salads: Drain salmon and discard marinade. Coat grill with cooking spray before heating grill to medium high. Place salmon on heated grill, skin side down; cover and cook for 15 to 20 minutes or until fish flakes easily with a fork. Meanwhile, in a large bowl, toss greens with well-shaken dressing to taste. Divide greens on dinner plates. Top with grilled salmon and citrus salsa to serve.

Sautéed Apple Crêpes
Makes 4 servings

Ingredients

2 large eggs, beaten
1 C. flour
1¼ C. milk
2 T. vegetable oil
¼ tsp. salt
1 T. butter
4 firm, tart apples, peeled, cored and sliced
Pinch of ground cinnamon
Powdered sugar, optional
Whipped cream, optional

Instructions

In a large bowl, blend together first five ingredients until mixture is the consistency of heavy cream. Refrigerate for 1 hour. Add milk if batter has thickened. In a preheated crêpe pan or nonstick 8″ to 9″ skillet, pour scant ¼ cup batter in, tilting pan to spread mixture evenly over the bottom of the pan. Cook over medium heat until crêpe is dry on top. Turn crêpe to cook the other side for 15 to 20 seconds. Stack cooked crêpes; wrap cooled crêpes tightly in plastic until ready to use. In a large skillet over medium heat, melt butter. Add sliced apples, sauté until soft and sprinkle with cinnamon. Spoon warm apples onto the center of each blintz; roll edges up and over from either side. If desired, dust with powdered sugar and top with whipped cream.

Coffee with Chocolate Caramel Syrup

Makes approximately 1½ cups syrup

Ingredients

½ C. heavy whipping cream
½ C. light corn syrup
¼ C. sugar
¼ C. brown sugar
Pinch of salt
4 oz. milk chocolate, chopped
2 T. butter
Brewed coffee
Whipped cream, optional
Chocolate shavings, optional

Instructions

In a small saucepan, stir together cream, corn syrup, both sugars and salt. Over medium-high heat, bring mixture to a rolling boil; reduce heat and continue to simmer for 8 to 10 minutes until smooth. Pour hot coffee in cups and stir in sauce to taste. If desired, top with whipped cream and chocolate shavings.

Chicken with Berry Sauce

Washington is filled with berries, both wild and cultivated. Picked in the woods or at a pick-your-own farm, or purchased at the farmers markets, blackberries, raspberries huckleberries, blueberries, strawberries and others find their way to the seattle table.

Makes 4 to 6 servings

Ingredients

1 C. unsweetened raspberry or strawberry puree
1 C. unsweetened raspberry juice
⅓ C. raspberry vinegar
1 T. soy sauce
2 T. Dijon mustard
1 T. fresh thyme leaves
1 tsp. ground black pepper
¼ C. finely chopped fresh basil
6 boneless, skinless chicken breast halves, pounded to even thickness
½ T. vegetable oil
4 to 6 fresh basil leaves for garnish

Instructions

In a large sealable plastic bag, combine first eight ingredients. Add chicken, seal and turn to coat; chill for 1 hour. Remove chicken and pat dry with paper towels. In a large skillet over medium-high heat, brown chicken breasts in heated oil for 2 minutes on each side. Reduce heat, add marinade to pan, cover and continue to cook for 3 to 4 minutes or until cooked through. Arrange breasts on a serving platter, spoon sauce over meat and garnish with basil leaves to serve.

Food for Thought

- Oysters and salmon have long been favorites in the area, as Native Americans enjoyed their plentiful availability long before Europeans arrived.

- Chinese influence on cuisine in the region was significant. Many workers came to the U.S. from China to build the cross-country railroads. When building was complete, many settled at the end of the line, in Seattle.

- Seattle is a coffee lover's dream location to enjoy a cup of fresh brew. It might have been the cool damp climate that made the drink a favorite in the city, but regardless of the reason, Seattle has become home to the three largest coffee chains in the U.S.

- A plethora of farmers markets are found throughout the city and state, where a wide variety of fresh produce can be purchased.

- Washington's oldest apple orchards are well over 100 years old. Trees were planted by settlers seeking to earn a living by farming. Apple production is a leading industry of the state (fruits are sold world-wide), and the Washington State Apple Blossom Festival has been celebrated for almost a century.

- World-renowned wineries are found in Washington; hundreds of wineries produce excellent red and white wines. Small-vineyard charm means that you may even meet the vintners as you tour the Washington Wine Country.

While in the Area

- View the city from the sky when you have lunch at the Space Needle. The iconic structure opened its doors on the first day of the 1962 World's Fair in Seattle. The top of the structure revolves 360 degrees, providing a magnificent view.

- Buy fresh fish at Pike Place Market, a major attraction with more than 200 businesses providing fresh produce, the catch of the day and more. You are likely to be entertained by street musicians as you select fresh flowers, handmade cheese or local wines.

- Take a harbor cruise or ride ferry boats in Puget Sound, where your eyes will be opened to the sweet views of the city, green shorelines and the Olympic and Cascade Mountains.

Nome, Alaska
Romantic Nights, Northern Lights

Candlelight Dinner for Two
Apple, Walnut & Blue Cheese Salad
Grilled Surf & Turf featuring:
Salmon Fillets *with*
Creamy Horseradish Sauce
and
Marinated Steak – Moose, Venison or Beef
Slow Cooker Wild Rice with Blueberries
Individual Baked Alaska

About your Destination

Welcome to Alaska, a land with sparse
population and vast wilderness and resources.
Alaska has more than 3 million lakes, 3,000
rivers, a dozen of the highest U.S. mountain
peaks, over 600 officially named glaciers
and another estimated 100,000 unnamed.
Additionally, its crisp coastal waters, forests
and tundra, islands, fiords, caves and waterfalls
make it the ultimate destination for outdoor
enthusiasts and nature lovers. Climb or ski the
mountains, kayak the streams, fish the waters
or photograph the scenery or animals such
as grizzly bears, reindeer, musk ox, sea lions,
whales and bald eagles.

continued

Apple, Walnut & Blue Cheese Salad

Makes 4 servings

Ingredients

1 egg white
½ C. walnut halves or pieces
2 T. sugar
5 T. cider vinegar
1 T. honey
1 T. Dijon mustard
1 T. finely minced green onions
5 T. olive oil
6 C. fresh salad greens
¾ C. crumbled blue cheese
2 apples, cored and diced

Instructions

Preheat oven to 350°F. In a small bowl, whisk egg white until foamy. Add walnuts and toss to coat. Transfer to a clean container and toss with sugar to coat. Bake in a single layer on a baking sheet for 10 minutes or until toasted; set aside to cool. In a medium bowl, whisk together vinegar, honey, mustard and green onions. Gradually add oil while whisking. In a large bowl, toss greens with dressing. Divide greens between serving plates and top with blue cheese, diced apples and toasted walnuts to serve.

continued from page 116

Native peoples, such as the Tlingit, Aleut, Inupiat and Yup'ik made their homes in Alaska long before the U.S. purchased it from Russia in 1867 for 7.2 million dollars, or about two cents per acre. Alaska has been divided into five large regions and broken into smaller subregions. In the Western Arctic sub-region of the Far North, the city of Nome lies along the Bering Sea. Nome's plentiful wildlife, rich gold rush history, and colorful, sweeping views make it a perfect Alaskan escape for daytime exploration or romantic evenings by the fire.

Theme & Setting

A romantic night under the Northern Lights is in store for you as you visit The Last Frontier. The wonder of Aurora Borealis is displayed as faintly glowing bands of colorful lights hung like dramatic curtains in the sky, rippling in the wind. Solar particles are blown into the earth's magnetic field and then bent by its force, more than 60 miles above the earth's surface.

Aurora Borealis includes greenish-yellow, faint blue, and even blood red curtains of colors. A shimmering tablecloth or runner with one or more of these deep colors will reflect candlelight. Use taper and votive candles to create the romantic effect of the Northern Lights right on your table. Decorative mirror tiles or trays will reflect even more candlelight. Relax with an after-dinner drink in front of the fire on a bear-skin rug for additional Alaskan atmosphere.

Salmon Fillets with Creamy Horseradish Sauce

Makes 2 servings

Ingredients for sauce
¼ C. sour cream
1½ T. mayonnaise
2 tsp. prepared horseradish
1 T. chopped fresh basil
1 tsp. fresh lemon juice
½ tsp. soy sauce
Salt and pepper to taste

Ingredients for salmon
Nonstick cooking spray
1 T. vegetable oil
1 tsp. prepared horseradish
1 tsp. soy sauce
¼ tsp. minced garlic
⅛ tsp. salt
Dash of ground black pepper
2 (6 oz.) salmon fillets, about 1" thick

Instructions
To make sauce: In a small bowl, whisk together all sauce ingredients and season with salt and pepper. Cover and chill. (Sauce can be prepared up to one day ahead.) **To make salmon:** Spray grill rack generously with nonstick spray. Preheat grill to medium-high. In a small bowl, whisk together oil, horseradish, soy sauce, garlic, salt and pepper. Brush mixture over both sides of salmon fillets. Grill salmon for about 4 minutes per side or until opaque in the center. Transfer salmon to plates and garnish with horseradish sauce to serve.

Alaska Quick Facts

Date of Statehood:	January 3, 1959
Population:	626,932
Capital:	Juneau
State Bird:	Willow Ptarmigan
State Flower:	Forget-me-not
State Nickname:	Golden State

Marinated Steak – Moose, Venison or Beef

Makes 2 servings

Ingredients

3 T. canola or vegetable oil
1 T. lemon juice
1 T. Worcestershire sauce
1 T. soy sauce
1½ tsp. minced garlic
½ tsp. ground black pepper
2 (7 to 8 oz.) moose, venison
   or beef steaks

Instructions

In a small bowl, whisk together oil, lemon juice, Worcestershire sauce, soy sauce, garlic, and pepper. Place steaks in a large sealable plastic bag and pour mixture over steaks; seal and toss gently to coat. Lay sealed bag in a shallow dish, placing steaks in a single layer to marinade evenly. Refrigerate a minimum of 4 hours, turning every half hour. Preheat grill to medium-high. Drain and discard marinade. Grill steaks for about 2 minutes per side to sear edges, sealing in juices; move steak to cooler portion of grill, reduce heat to medium-low and continue to grill to desired doneness. Transfer steak to a covered dish to help seal in juices, just until served.

Slow Cooker Wild Rice with Blueberries

Blueberries are known to be rich in antioxidants, but the wild blueberries of Alaska have even higher rates than commercially grown varieties. In Alaska, fresh Blue Huckleberries, Dwarf Blueberries, Bog Blueberries and Alaska Blueberries are ripe for the picking.

Makes 2 large servings

Ingredients

¾ C. uncooked wild rice
1½ tsp. butter
¼ tsp. salt
⅛ tsp. ground black pepper
2 green onions, sliced
1 (14 oz.) can vegetable broth
½ (4 oz.) can sliced mushrooms,
   drained
¼ C. toasted slivered almonds*
¼ C. dried blueberries

Instructions

In a 2- to 3-quart slow cooker, combine rice, butter, salt, pepper, green onions, broth and mushrooms. Cover and cook on low for 4 to 5 hours or until rice is tender. Stir almonds and blueberries into rice mixture. Cover and continue to cook on low for 15 minutes. Fluff with fork before serving.

To toast, place almonds in a single layer on a baking sheet. Bake at 350°F for approximately 5 to 10 minutes or until almonds are golden brown.

Individual Baked Alaska

Although this sweet treat did not originate in Alaska, and variations of it were served long before the purchase of the land, the dish was "created" by Delmonico's Restaurant in New York City in honor of the newly acquired territory.

<u>Makes 2 servings</u>

Ingredients

Pound cake, purchased
   or homemade
Ice cream of your choice
2 egg whites
⅛ tsp. cream of tartar
4 T. sugar

Instructions

Slice 2 pieces of pound cake, ½˝ thick. With a 3˝ round cookie cutter, make 2 rounds of pound cake; place on a baking sheet. Place a large scoop* of ice cream on top of each round, pressing down lightly to hold it in place. Freeze cake and ice cream for at least 1 hour until ice cream is very hard. Before serving, prepare the meringue. In a large mixing bowl, beat egg whites on medium speed until frothy. Add cream of tartar, increase speed and beat until soft peaks form. Add sugar, 1 tablespoon at a time, and continue to beat until stiff peaks form. Preheat oven to 500°F.** Remove cake and ice cream from the freezer and transfer to a broiler pan. Using a spoon, quickly spread the meringue evenly over the ice cream, covering it completely, fully meeting the edge of the cake. Bake for about 2 minutes or just until meringue is lightly browned. Remove from oven, transfer to dessert plate and serve immediately.

If a large ice cream scoop is not available, line a punch cup or similar mold with plastic wrap and press ice cream into it; pull out plastic to unmold the ice cream ball.

**Special equipment, such as a salamander or culinary torch, is used to brown the tops of food. Instead of using an oven in this recipe, one of these culinary tools could be used to toast the meringue.*

Food for Thought

- Super-size vegetables grow in Alaska, where the intense almost-around-the-clock sunshine is more beneficial than the short growing season is detrimental. Examples include Brussels sprouts as large as apples and zucchini as big as baseball bats. These unique vegetables won't be found in stores in the lower 48 states, as Alaska only produces about two percent of their food, requiring the import rather than export of crops.

- Locally grown produce includes many root vegetables such as carrots, potatoes, turnips and onions, since they store well through the long winter season. Additionally cabbage, lettuce greens, tomatoes, squash, rhubarb, apples and berries are popular.

- Native families, as well as other Alaskans, gather berries, fish the waters and hunt the lands for food provisions. Moose stew is just one of Alaska's wild game traditions.

- Sourdough bread is common in Alaska. It was made popular during gold mining days as miners headed to isolated claims with their sourdough starter. They ate so much sourdough that the prospector was soon being called a "sourdough."

While in the Area

- Pan for gold near Nome where evidence of the Alaskan gold rush is plentiful, including abandoned dredges, steam engines, old mining claims and old railroad tracks.

- Learn about the native people who live in the area. Commonly known as Eskimos, they often prefer to be called by their specific tribal names. The term Eskimo is often used broadly for many northern tribes since it means "eaters of raw meat." The Carrie M. McLain Memorial Museum presents the art and lifestyle of the natives with rare artifacts and photos.

- Watch for the winning dog team of the 1,049-mile Iditarod Sled Dog Race to cross the finish line. The race starts in Anchorage on the first Saturday in March, with the winner arriving at the finish line in Nome about nine days later.

Index

Salsa Verde (Green Chile Sauce)	New Mexico	82
Slow Cooker Marinated Mushrooms	California	101
Slow-Cooked Apple Butter	Kentucky	47
Sonoma Stuffed Dates	California	101
Spring Crab Dip	Maine	3
Texas Caviar	Texas	75
Tomato & Olive Bruschetta	California	102
Walnut & Port Wine Cheese Apples	California	100

Breads & Breakfast

Cheese Grits	Kentucky	45
Cinnamon Raisin Biscuits	Kentucky	47
Corn Muffins with Honey Butter	Georgia	58
Country Scrambled Eggs	Kentucky	46
Hopi Blue Corn Hotcakes with Sweet Peaches	Arizona	90
Jalapeño Cornbread	Texas	76
Maple-Glazed Breakfast Ham	Kentucky	46
New Mexican Breakfast Burrito	New Mexico	84
No-Knead Overnight Dinner Rolls	Pennsylvania	16
Spoon Bread	Virginia	53
Spring French Baguette	Washington	111

Soups & Salads

Apple, Walnut & Blue Cheese Salad	Alaska	117
Best Broccoli Salad	Pennsylvania	15
Chuckwagon Wheel Pasta Salad	Wyoming	106
Easy Texas Chili	Texas	77
Georgia Peach & Summer Fruit Salad	Georgia	57
German Potato Salad	Wisconsin	29
Great American Macaroni Salad	Missouri	39
Hawaiian Fruit Salad	Hawaii	94

Ma's Coleslaw	New Mexico	83
Michigan Tangy Coleslaw	Michigan	21
Oyster Stew of the Northwest	Washington	112
Peanut Soup	Virginia	52
Salad of the South with Creole Honey Mustard Vinaigrette	Louisiana	69
Salmon Citrus Salad	Washington	112
Southwestern Black Bean Soup	Arizona	88
Spiced Peach Salad	Wyoming	105
Spinach Salad with Blueberry Dressing	Maine	5
Sweet Potato Salad	Georgia	59
Virginia Crab Salad	Virginia	52
Wisconsin Beer Cheese Soup	Wisconsin	28

Vegetables & Side Dishes

Aloha Sweet Potatoes	Hawaii	95
Chile Con Queso Fries	New Mexico	83
Classic Cream Corn Bake	Missouri	41
Cookie's Roasted Potatoes	Wyoming	107
Corn on the Cob-on-a-Stick	Iowa	35
Creamed Pearl Onions	Virginia	54
Creamy Baked Macaroni & Cheese	Michigan	23
Easiest Hot Applesauce	Michigan	22
Escalloped Potatoes	Pennsylvania	17
Jazzed-Up BBQ Beans	Missouri	41
Lemon Roasted Baby Carrots & Potatoes	Massachusetts	11
Mesa Summer Squash & Corn	Arizona	90
Slow Cooker Wild Rice with Blueberries	Alaska	119

Meats & Main Dishes

Baked BBQ Chicken Wings	Wyoming	106
Burgers of the Southwest	New Mexico	81

Chicken with Berry Sauce	Washington	114
Cuban Sandwiches	Florida	65
Farmer's Meatloaf	Pennsylvania	16
Hot Beef Sundae	Iowa	34
Indian Fry Bread Tacos	Arizona	89
Italian Shrimp Skewers	California	101
Jambalaya of the Delta	Louisiana	71
K.C. BBQ Ribs	Missouri	40
Lobster Club with Lemon Mayo	Maine	4
Macadamia Nut-Crusted Mahi Mahi	Hawaii	94
Marinated Steak – Moose, Venison or Beef	Alaska	119
Nantucket Baked Cod	Massachusetts	10
Oven-Fried Picnic Chicken	Georgia	58
Pan-Fried Trout	Michigan	22
Salmon Fillets with Creamy Horseradish Sauce	Alaska	118
Savory Beef Brisket	Wyoming	107
Slow Cooker Kalua Pig - Pulled Pork	Hawaii	95
Spiced Apple Pork Roast	Virginia	53
Wisconsin Beer Brats	Wisconsin	28

Desserts

All-American Cherry Pie	Michigan	23
Amish Caramel Corn	Pennsylvania	18
Banana & Macadamia Cakes with White Chocolate Sauce	Hawaii	96
Beignets (Donuts)	Louisiana	72
Blackberry Cobbler	Texas	77
Buttermilk Brownies	Missouri	42
Caramel Apples-on-a-Stick	Iowa	36
Fluffy Cranberry Mousse	Massachusetts	12
Fresh Orchard Apple Crisp	Wisconsin	30

Funnel Cakes	Iowa	36
Individual Baked Alaska	Alaska	120
Jonathan Apple Pie	Pennsylvania	17
Key Lime Tartlets	Florida	66
Mackinac Island Famous Fudge	Michigan	24
Needhams (Potato Candies)	Maine	5
Orange King's Cake	Virginia	54
Pecan Pie Squares	Georgia	60
Raisin Bread Pudding	Wyoming	108
Sautéed Apple Crêpes	Washington	113
Southern Girl Pralines	Louisiana	72
Whoopie Pies	Maine	6
Wine Poached Pears with Chocolate Drizzle	California	102